Contents

Acknowledgments

The authors and editor wish to thank the following individuals who contributed to the development of *Curious Crayons: Early Childhood Science in Living Color.*

Terrific Science Press Design and Production Team

Document Production Managers: Susan Gertz, Amy Stander
Production Coordinator: Dot Lyon
Technical Writing: Dot Lyon, Tom Schaffner
Technical Editing: Dot Lyon, Amy Stander
Production: Anita Winkler, Tom Schaffner, Dot Lyon
Photography: Susan Gertz, Tom Schaffner
Cover Design and Layout: Susan Gertz

Content Specialists, Reviewers, and Testers

Eva Facen, Teacher, Abilities First Early Childhood Learning Center, Middletown, OH

Stacy Francis, Director, Middletown Area Family YMCA Children's Center, Middletown, OH

Paula Liberatore, Director, Abilities First Early Childhood Learning Center, Middletown, OH

Lori Norton-Meier, Assistant Professor, Department of Curriculum and Instruction, Iowa State University, Ames, IA

Kristiana Reeves, Teacher, Middletown Area Family YMCA Children's Center, Middletown, OH

Teresa Reeves, Teacher, Middletown Area Family YMCA Children's Center, Middletown, OH

Rachael Shepherd, Teacher, Middletown Area Family YMCA Children's Center, Middletown, OH

Rebecca Shepherd, Teacher, Abilities First Early Childhood Learning Center, Middletown, OH

Foreword

Science is a way for children to explore, discover, and make sense of the world around them. When presented in a way that is meaningful for young minds, early science experiences provide the foundation for a lifetime of science learning both in and beyond school. Science learning is exploring, wondering, and discovering—it is not about memorizing facts.

The goal of the *Big Science for Little Hands* series is to help young children develop an understanding of basic concepts about the physical world and basic process skills that fit their level of learning development. How do children develop these concepts and skills? They need repeated personal experiences with materials and events from their everyday world. They explore materials, investigate ideas, and link what they discover with the world around them. *Curious Crayons: Early Childhood Science in Living Color* builds skills for a lifetime of learning.

I wish you and the future scientists, leaders, and informed citizens in your care great fun while learning with *Curious Crayons*. Enjoy!

Mickey Sarquis, Director
Terrific Science Programs
Miami University (Ohio)

Using This Book

This section explains the organization of the book and discusses early childhood learning, lesson planning, assessment, acquiring materials for the activities, safety, and setting up the classroom.

Organization of the Book

The book is organized in eight parts.

Parts 1–5 (learning cycle activities) contain 19 activities that address the four phases of the learning cycle: awareness, exploration, inquiry, and application. Advanced Inquiry activities are also included for children who are ready to experiment further. Each activity is presented in an easy-to-use format. (See pages 8–9 for details on activity format and pages 120–123 for a detailed discussion of learning cycles.)

Part 6: Crayons Across the Curriculum contains cross-curricular activities that relate the topic of crayons to writing, reading, math, biology, drama, and art. Teachers may choose to use one or more of these activities before, during, or after the learning cycle activities.

Part 7: Science for Young Learners contains information on developmentally-appropriate science instruction for young children, why we teach early childhood science, fundamental concepts and process skills, teaching with learning cycles, and documenting learning.

Part 8: All About Crayons and Wax presents interesting facts for teachers about the history of crayons, manufacture of crayons, and information about wax. Teachers may want to share some of this information with children.

Range of Learners

Because young children are unique individuals who progress at their own pace, they reach the various stages of intellectual, physical, emotional, and social development at different times. Some children will understand all or most of the fundamental concepts about the physical world presented in this book (see page 113 for details), and other children will understand only a few concepts or none at all.

Many children will be able to answer the straightforward questions included in the activities, but they are likely to have difficulty with the inquiry-style questions. With time and practice, children will become more comfortable with inquiry questions. Process and inquiry skills are challenging to young children, but they can learn these skills and build the foundation for a lifetime of science learning. (See Part 7: Science for Young Learners for a discussion of inquiry learning and teaching.)

Lesson Planning

Curious Crayons offers a large selection of activities. The activities are organized by the stages of the learning cycle. Our goal is to provide you with a number of activities at each stage so you can choose what works best for you. For example, teachers wanting to designate one week to learning about crayons can select one activity from each phase (four activities) plus one of the activities in the Crayons Across the Curriculum section of this book. You do not need to complete activities on consecutive days, although you should present the activities in learning cycle order (awareness, exploration, inquiry, and application).

If your class uses centers, you may wish to incorporate Crayons Across the Curriculum activities and other crayon experiences as ongoing activities over the duration of the unit. This will provide children with topic enrichment and reinforcement. Center activities might include:

Science Center
*   Since some crayons are made from honeycomb beeswax, place a chunk of honeycomb (sometimes called comb honey) in a clear plastic jar or bag. Provide magnifying lenses for a closer look.

Art Center
*   Make a variety of crayons and paper available for children to participate in creative coloring.
*   Offer chalk, washable markers, colored pencils, and paper. Ask children to trace different-sized crayons.
*   Do **Across the Curriculum 7: Sandpaper Printing**. Children create fabric art by first coloring on sandpaper.

Math Center
*   Offer rulers and tape measures so children can measure a variety of different-sized crayons.
*   Provide a balance and same-sized weights (such as centimeter/gram cubes or plastic counting bears) so children can weigh a variety of crayons.
*   Do **Across the Curriculum 5: What Are the Chances?** Children use crayons to make predictions.

Dress-Up/Housekeeping Center
*   Have children wear antenna made from pipe cleaners taped to construction paper headbands. Build beehives in the classroom as described in **Across the Curriculum 6: Buzzing About Bees**. Children will have fun being bees and collecting nectar!

Writing Center
*   Offer paper and crayons for children to draw and write their own crayon stories.
*   Do **Across the Curriculum 1: Writing to Learn**. Children create pictures and stories revealing what they learned about crayons.

Assessment

Collecting children's ideas over time is an important feature of ongoing assessment. Examining classroom work helps teachers to identify patterns of learning for individuals as well as groups of children. This process also helps a teacher reflect upon his or her own instructional practice. Teachers can collect samples of work as well as take photographs of and make notes about children's experiences as they work. These examples, photographs, and notes can be organized into a science journal for each child. (See Documenting Learning on pages 124–126 for a more in-depth discussion of collecting and evaluating evidence of learning.)

As discussed in Teaching with Learning Cycles on page 123, the activities in the application phase of the learning cycle can be used for an assessment at the end of the unit. Teachers may also wish to establish evaluation criteria based upon learning objectives such as the following:

- Child knows that crayons are made in factories.
- Child knows that crayons are made of wax.
- Child understands that crayon wax transfers to the paper during coloring.
- Child knows that crayon wax is waterproof.
- Child knows that crayons can melt.

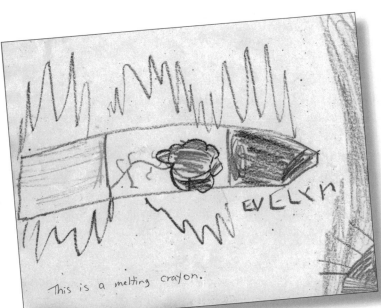

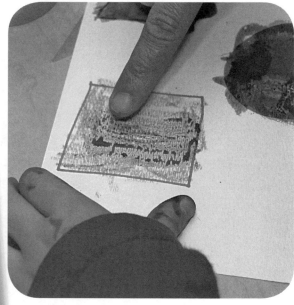

Teachers may use drawings like those above to discuss key features a student can identify about crayons and wax.

NAEYC Early Childhood Program Standards

This book addresses the following preschool and kindergarten NAEYC Early Children Program Standards for science cognitive development under Standard 2: Curriculum.

2.G.02 Children learn key content and principles of science such as structure and property of matter and behavior of materials.

2.G.03 Children use the five senses to observe, explore, and experiment with scientific phenomena.

2.G.04 Children use simple tools to observe objects and scientific phenomena.

2.G.05 Children collect data and represent and document their findings.

2.G.06 Children think, question, and reason about observed and inferred phenomena.

2.G.07 Children discuss scientific concepts in everyday conversation.

2.G.08 Children learn and use scientific terminology and vocabulary associated with the content areas.

National Science Education Standards

This book addresses the following Science Content Standards: K–4.

Science as Inquiry:

Abilities Necessary to Do Scientific Inquiry
- Ask a question about objects, organisms, and events in the environment.
- Plan and conduct a simple investigation.
- Employ simple equipment and tools to gather data and extend the senses.
- Use data to construct a reasonable explanation.
- Communicate investigations and explanations.

Understandings About Scientific Inquiry
- Scientific investigations involve asking and answering a question and comparing the answer with what scientists already know about the world.
- Simple instruments, such as magnifiers, thermometers, and rulers, provide more information than scientists obtain using only their senses.
- Scientists develop explanations using observations (evidence) and what they already know about the world (scientific knowledge). Good explanations are based on evidence from investigations.

Physical Science:

Properties of Objects and Materials

- Objects have many observable properties, including size, weight, shape, color, temperature, and the ability to react with other substances. Those properties can be measured using tools, such as rulers, balances, and thermometers.
- Objects are made of one or more materials, such as paper, wood, and metal. Objects can be described by the properties of the materials from which they are made, and those properties can be used to separate or sort a group of objects or materials.
- Materials can exist in different states—solid, liquid, and gas. Some common materials, such as water, can be changed from one state to another by heating or cooling.

Science and Technology:

Understanding about Science and Technology

- Tools help scientists make better observations, measurements, and equipment for investigations. They help scientists see, measure, and do things that they could not otherwise see, measure, and do.

A Collection of Crayons and Wax

To begin this unit, you will need to collect a variety of crayons. The children will be observing these crayons with their senses and using the crayons during hands-on classroom activities. Choose some familiar examples of crayons as well as some new types. Look for crayons with different smells, textures, sizes, shapes, and colors. There are many types of crayons, including regular size, large size, flat-sided, scented, glitter, neon, metallic, twistable, erasable, glow-in-the-dark, and multicultural. Try to include crayons from different companies in your selection.

Consider the age and experience of your children as you build your collection. Younger children and those building basic experience benefit from a small variety of crayons. Older children and those with more background may enjoy a wider crayon selection with more subtle differences. As the children become more familiar with crayon characteristics, add new samples to challenge their learning. Opportunities are included for children and adults to hunt for crayons and wax products at home.

Keep in mind that a few activities involve matching the crayons into pairs or groups. Your crayon collection should have enough variety to make these matching activities interesting.

Be Safe

Emphasize safety rules with the children while doing the activities. Remind children not to put crayons and other objects in their mouths, ears, or near eyes. Children should keep crayons off the floor because stepped-on crayons may roll and be unsafe. Children should also be reminded of the additional safety issues listed with each activity.

Setting Up the Learning Environment

Choose an area for children to work where you can easily monitor children's involvement and where children can freely explore the materials. Good traffic flow will help children focus on their work.

Since some activities involve quantities of crayons, consider the best way to store the crayons so they are visible and accessible to young scientists but don't roll away. Be wary of supplying so many crayons and other materials that the work area becomes too crowded and children have problems focusing on specific items. As classroom space allows, designate areas to display crayon and wax collections, class charts, and children's work.

Helpful Hint

Placing crayons on trays, paper plates, plastic bins, or aluminum pie pans helps children organize their work space while investigating crayons.

The Social Context

Learning in the early years takes place in a social context. The cooperation and collaboration that begin in these years are important qualities for learners of all ages. Build in opportunities for children to practice these skills. For example, sharing must be practiced in a variety of situations with different people. Encourage children to help each other while working together. They will discover more when they hear different perspectives and ideas. Children will gain experience in listening respectfully to others' ideas. Fostering these experiences involves a working noise level in your classroom. Working noise does not offend others or interrupt them, but it shows that people are working and developing new ideas. Maintaining a reasonable noise level shows that children respect others who are working in the classroom.

Choose materials to encourage social interaction. Some procedures may work better when several children share a task. Sometimes a limited number of materials will encourage children to share with others and set up systems to cooperate. Reflect upon the role social learning has in your classroom and choose how you want to foster this learning in your activities.

Format of Activities

Each activity is presented in an easy-to-use format.

Learning Cycle Phase
Identifies the activity's learning cycle phase. (Details about each phase are discussed in Teaching with Learning Cycles on pages 120–123.)

Activity Title
Identifies the overall goal or theme of the activity.

Activity Introduction
Briefly describes the activity.

Duration
Provides an estimate of the classroom time and group size recommended for the activity.

Purpose
States the skills children will use and develop during the activity.

What You Need
Lists the materials needed to do the activity.

Be Safe
States relevant safety issues to be aware of during the activity.

Getting Ready
Provides teachers with instructions for preparing materials prior to the activity (when applicable).

Spotlight Vocabulary
Lists vocabulary words that teachers may want to introduce or reinforce during the activity.

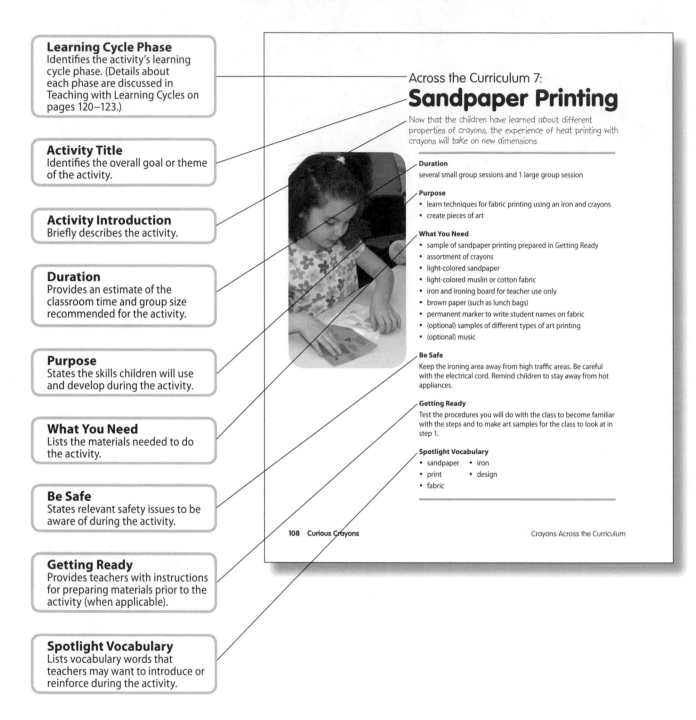

Across the Curriculum 7:
Sandpaper Printing

Now that the children have learned about different properties of crayons, the experience of heat printing with crayons will take on new dimensions.

Duration
several small group sessions and 1 large group session

Purpose
- learn techniques for fabric printing using an iron and crayons
- create pieces of art

What You Need
- sample of sandpaper printing prepared in Getting Ready
- assortment of crayons
- light-colored sandpaper
- light-colored muslin or cotton fabric
- iron and ironing board for teacher use only
- brown paper (such as lunch bags)
- permanent marker to write student names on fabric
- (optional) samples of different types of art printing
- (optional) music

Be Safe
Keep the ironing area away from high traffic areas. Be careful with the electrical cord. Remind children to stay away from hot appliances.

Getting Ready
Test the procedures you will do with the class to become familiar with the steps and to make art samples for the class to look at in step 1.

Spotlight Vocabulary
- sandpaper
- print
- fabric
- iron
- design

Crayons Across the Curriculum

Begin ────

1. Review the fact that crayons are made of wax and that coloring with crayons causes the wax to rub off the crayon and stick to the object being colored. Tell the children that you wonder if crayons will color on different kinds of paper. Show children the class chart (prepared in Getting Ready) and discuss what materials you want them to try coloring.

2. Have the children work in pairs. (Working with partners will encourage children to talk about their experiment and share ideas.) Give each person either squares of test materials or a test board you prepared in Getting Ready. Ask each child to color on the different paper using the same crayon. (You may want to give one partner a light-colored crayon and one a dark-colored crayon.)

Helpful Hint

When doing hands-on activities with the children, try to use "I wonder…" statements often to reinforce the way scientists think. Modeling the use of "I wonder…" throughout the unit should make **Advanced Inquiry 2: I Wonder…** easier for the children to do.

Helpful Hint

You may need to give children clues about how to work in pairs. Watch for successful pairs and share their strategies with the class. Do the partners take turns sharing ideas? How do the partners help each other? How do the partners offer their ideas to each other? How do the partners share materials?

Questions to facilitate the processes of observing:
> *What do you notice about coloring on different paper?*
> *What do you hear and see?*
> *How do your results compare to your partner's results? What is the same? What is different?*

Seen and heard:
  Children said, "It works" and "The cardboard is noisy."

Continue ────

4. Gather the class together to discuss their observations. Encourage the children to look at their test materials and explain what they noticed. Record their observations on the class chart.

Questions to facilitate the discussion:
> *What do you notice about coloring on different paper?*
> *Does the crayon wax stick to all kinds of paper?*
> *Which papers were hardest to color?…easiest to color?*

5. Give the children additional time for free exploration. For example, put samples of the same and different types of paper in the science center with different types of crayons. The children may have new ideas to explore.

6. Display the class chart so children and adults can review the results.

What to Look For

Observe how children work cooperatively and collaboratively during this activity. These skills help children focus on and extend their discoveries. Listen for children to notice ways that the paper changes with color. Encourage children to observe how wax sticks to materials having different textures. Children should notice the sound made when coloring across the ridges of corrugated cardboard. Crayons can color on many different materials, but seem to color more easily on textured materials (such as construction paper and newspaper) than on smooth materials (such as vellum).

Begin
Lists procedures to begin the activity.

Helpful Hint Sidebar
Offers teacher tips to enhance or extend the activity.

Guiding Questions
Includes suggested questions to ask children to facilitate the building of process and inquiry skills.

Seen and Heard
Lists examples of children's comments and reactions.

Continue
Lists additional procedures to continue the activity.

What to Look For
Offers children's reactions that indicate understanding of the topic.

Process Skill Power Sidebar
Presents information about fundamental process skills that are emphasized in the activity.

Process Skill Power

"Comparing is a powerful process that can lead to the understanding of many important scientific ideas."

"Organizing is the process of putting objects or phenomena together on the basis of a logical rationale."

Lawrence Lowery, 1992

Part 1: Awareness

What is the awareness phase?

The awareness phase provides children with experiences to help them develop a broad recognition of and interest in objects, people, events, or concepts.

During awareness, children

- experience,
- awaken curiosity, and
- develop an interest.

The teacher's role is to

- create a rich environment;
- provide opportunities by introducing new objects, people, events, or concepts;
- invite and encourage interest by posing a problem or question;
- respond to children's interest; and
- show interest and enthusiasm.

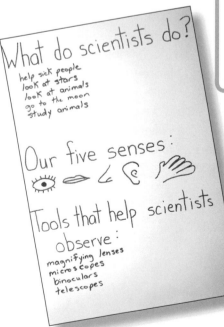

What do scientists do?

help sick people
look at stars
look at animals
go to the moon
study animals

Our five senses:

Tools that help scientists observe:

magnifying lenses
microscopes
binoculars
telescopes

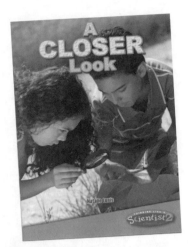

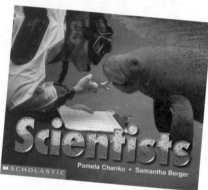

Awareness 1:
Taking a Closer Look at Science

Children explore tools that scientists use to observe and find out more about the world.

Duration

1 large group session and independent exploration

Purpose

- share ideas about tools scientists use to observe and gather information
- compare prior knowledge about scientists' tools with information in a children's book

What You Need

- poster board or large piece of paper
- index cards
- scissors
- *A Closer Look,* by Newbridge Educational Publishing; *Scientists,* by Pamela Chanko and Samantha Berger; or similar resource
- ⌦ A Closer Look *may be difficult to find. It is available for purchase online at* www.newbridgeonline.com. *Although the student book version can be read to the class, the larger pictures in the big book version make viewing much easier.*
- magnifying lenses
- other equipment scientists use, such as simple pocket microscopes, binoculars, rulers, balances, and clipboards with paper and pencils
- ⌦ *Battery-operated pocket microscopes are available in stores and from online suppliers that sell electrical and scientific devices (such as Radio Shack®). If you have access to traditional microscopes and telescopes, the children could benefit from seeing these tools.*

Getting Ready

- Prepare a class chart as shown at left.
- Prepare index cards as shown at right, one for each pair of children.

Example of class chart

What do scientists do?

Our five senses:

Tools that help scientists observe:

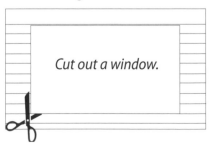

Cut out a window.

Spotlight Vocabulary

- scientist
- tool
- magnify
- observe
- observation words (such as smooth, bumpy, speckled)
- measuring words (such as compare, size, weigh)
- recording words (such as write, draw, list)

Begin

1. Tell the children that a scientist observes, predicts, does experiments, and makes conclusions based on their findings. Give children examples of scientists, such as chemists, zoologists, astronauts, and astronomers. Ask the children, "What do these scientists do?" Record their answers on the class chart prepared in Getting Ready.

2. Explain that we can learn a lot about the world around us by observing with our five senses. Ask the children to name the five senses. Make a list of their ideas on the class chart and help them to give examples. Explain that the five senses are tools scientists have with them all the time.

3. Ask children what other tools (equipment) help scientists better observe things in the world. Record their ideas on the class chart. (Don't worry if the children can't name many tools. You will revisit the list in step 5.)

4. Read *A Closer Look, Scientists,* or similar resource to the class. Ask children to identify the observation tools they recognize. Encourage them to explain how those tools can help scientists find out new information.

   Questions to guide children's thinking:

   > *What could help a scientist make better observations?*

   > *Have you seen this scientist's tool? (Point to a picture in the book.)*

   > *Where have you seen this tool?*

   > *How does a scientist use this tool?*

   > *How could this help scientists learn more?*

Helpful Hint

You can start a "word wall" for all new vocabulary words. Add new words to the wall before doing each new activity. Revisit the wall often.

Helpful Hint

Our five senses are:
- sight
- hearing
- touch
- smell
- taste

5. Return to the class chart. Ask the children what ideas they would like to add to the list of tools that help scientists observe. Highlight tools that children could use in the classroom. Display the class chart so children and adults can review the results.

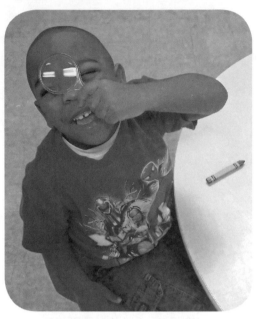

Continue

6. Show the children some basic science tools that they can use in the classroom to enhance their observations. Introduce the children to magnifying lenses. Because these tools are often used incorrectly, have a child demonstrate how to use a magnifying lens correctly. (See Helpful Hints at top left.)

Children often use magnifying lenses incorrectly.

7. Have children work in pairs to practice observing with magnifying lenses. Each pair should have a magnifying lens and an index card prepared in Getting Ready. One child should choose an object in the classroom and put the index card frame on the object to help the observer concentrate. The other child (the observer) should practice looking at the object with the magnifying lens. Have partners take turns so they both choose an object and observe with the magnifying lens. Then, ask children to draw pictures showing what they saw with their eyes and with the magnifying lenses.

8. Provide opportunities for independent exploration and role play by allowing the children to use magnifying lenses and other science equipment. Subsequently, children can draw pictures of scientists—or themselves—using the equipment.

Questions to guide interest:

> *Why do scientists use magnifying lenses?*

> *What kinds of objects would be good to study with a magnifying lens?*

> *How do science tools help you learn?*

Seen and heard:

Children said, "Scientists look at things" and "Whoa, it gets bigger!"

What to Look For

While some children will easily be able to vocalize their descriptions of what scientists do, others may have difficultly putting their ideas into words. Look for opportunities to encourage all children to participate. Showing pictures in the book you read to the class should help children describe their ideas.

While the children may not understand the meaning of process skill words such as "observe," "measure," or "record," they can learn to associate these terms with what scientists do. Look for children to use common synonyms for process skills (as indicated in the Spotlight Vocabulary) when talking about what scientists do.

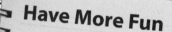

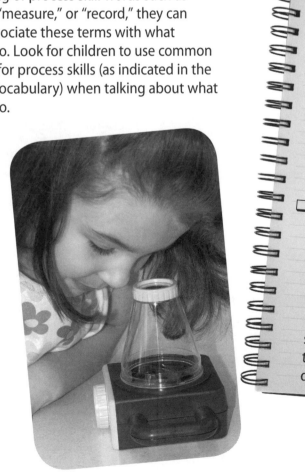

Introduce children to the fact that scientists are always looking for more to learn. From the book you read in step 4 or another source, show children pictures of scientists at work and ask what each scientist might be wondering about. For example, an astronomer looking into a telescope might be wondering what a star looks like. By pointing out what different scientists wonder about, you are preparing the children to wonder about many exciting things during the inquiry phase of the learning cycle.

Have More Fun

❑ Help children explore with a pocket microscope. These microscopes are put right on the objects being observed. Many pocket microscopes magnify at 32x—some go up to 100x. Offer interesting objects to look at, such as leaves, newspaper print, photographs, sand, and dirt. Help younger children focus on the object by turning the knob.

❑ Let a small group of children explore with binoculars or telescopes to look at things far away. Children can make their own binoculars with two toilet paper tubes taped together and a string handle. These do not magnify, but help children focus their observations in a small area. Hopefully the children can tell you how toilet paper binoculars differ from regular binoculars.

Awareness 2:
Getting Curious About Crayons

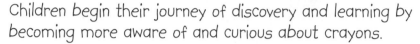

Children begin their journey of discovery and learning by becoming more aware of and curious about crayons.

Duration

1 large group session, 1 small group session, and independent exploration

Purpose

- become interested in and aware of different kinds of crayons
- begin comparing similarities and differences
- develop observation skills

What You Need

- different types of crayons
- 👉 *There are many types of crayons, including regular size, large size, flat-sided, scented, glitter, neon, metallic, twistable, erasable, glow-in-the-dark, and multicultural. Try to include crayons from different companies in your selection.*
- magnifying lenses

Spotlight Vocabulary

- crayon
- observe
- shape words (such as cylinder, rectangle, flat)
- size words (such as long, short, thick, thin)
- color words (such as white, brown, red, green)
- descriptive words (such as shiny, smooth)

Begin

1. Explain to the class that they will be exploring some common objects that they have probably seen and used before. However, some of the objects may be new to them. Emphasize that these objects are for science and are to be studied, not to be put into mouths. Pass around an assortment of crayons so that each child gets a chance to touch, smell, and observe several types. Let children take a small collection to observe with a partner. (Working with partners encourages science talking, cooperation, and the development of ideas.)

Questions to guide interest and enthusiasm:

> *What do you notice about these objects? Use your senses but don't put the objects in your mouth.*

> *Where have you seen these objects?*

> *How do people use them?*

Seen and heard:

Children said, "It has words on them," "Grandma gave me a big, big, big box of crayons for my birthday," and "They color."

2. Now have the children observe their crayons using the magnifying lenses. Encourage children to talk with a partner about what they observe.

Helpful Hint

Children will use magnifying lenses many times during the activities in this book, so make sure they use this tool correctly. (See **Awareness 1: Taking a Closer Look at Science** for how-to instructions.)

Questions to guide interest and enthusiasm:

> *What do you notice about the objects now that you used the magnifying lens?*

> *Why do people use magnifying lenses?*

> *What new observations have you made?*

Seen and heard:

Children said, "I found a hole," "I see sparkles," and "Now my crayon is bigger."

3. Tell children that some of these objects will be left in the room for them to observe and use.

Continue

4. Place a variety of crayons and paper in areas of the room and let the children freely explore. Make sure to include what may be needed for each crayon type (for example, extra erasers for the erasable crayons and black paper for the metallic crayons). Suggested locations include the art easel, housekeeping area, science center, and math center. You may want to include some crayons in their original boxes.

5. Meet with the children in small groups and tell them you are going to create a class book about the crayon samples they have explored. Using one page for each child, ask each child to share what he or she discovered about the crayons. For example, you can ask what the magnifying lens helped discover or you can ask where crayons were found in the classroom. Use drawings rather than words whenever possible so nonreaders will understand the information.

6. Assemble the pages into a picture book. This class book can be used to introduce **Exploration 1: A Closer Look at Crayons.**

What to Look For

Watch for increased curiosity and interest as children use, explore, and talk about crayons. Try to encourage and show enthusiasm.

Awareness 3:
The Crayon-Making Process

Children receive an overview of how and where crayons are made.

Duration

1 large group session

Purpose

- discover what materials make up crayons
- learn how crayons are made in factories
- gain background for upcoming activities involving crayons

What You Need

- *Wax to Crayons,* by Inez Snyder, or similar resource

Spotlight Vocabulary

- crayon
- wax
- mold
- powder
- label
- worker
- factory
- melt

Begin

1. Review with the class what they have learned so far. Explain that crayons are made by workers in factories. Ask the children to name other things that may be made in factories.

   ### Seen and heard:

   Children said, "There's a chocolate factory," "My mommy works in a factory," and "I wish my daddy worked in a crayon factory so he could get me some!"

Continue

2. Read *Wax to Crayons* or a similar resource to the class. Ask the children to describe what they see in the pictures. Explain concepts that may be confusing. Tell the class that later they will be doing exciting activities with crayons.

Let's Sing

Crayons
(sung to the tune of Mary Had a Little Lamb)

Crayons are made in fact-or-ies

Fact-or-ies

Fact-or-ies

Crayons are made in fact-or-ies

So we can draw and color.

Questions to guide the discussion:

> *What is used to make crayons?*

> *How do crayons get their shape?*

> *Where are crayons made?*

Seen and heard:

> *Children said, "It looks like butter," "It's cooking," and "I wish we could make crayons."*

Student drawing about visiting a crayon factory from
Crayons Across the Curriculum 1: Writing to Learn.

Have More Fun

❑ If you have a computer in the classroom, check out *www.crayola.com*. Children can play games, color pictures, and see how crayons are made. The website also contains creative crafts and lesson plans for families and teachers.

❑ A movie showing how crayons are made is available online at *pbskids. org/rogers/R_house/picpic.htm*. This website is a Mr. Rogers/PBS site and is appropriate for young children. Photographs and accompanying activities are also included.

Stop and Reflect

Review with the children how and why scientists use magnifying lenses in their jobs. Review where children have seen both magnifying lenses and crayons—at home, in their community, and in the classroom.

Guide the reflection process by asking

- What can you do to work like a scientist?
- What have you noticed about crayons?
- What could we do to find out more about crayons?

Encourage children to use their own words to describe the process skills they use to work like scientists. For example, a child may say that he or she "looks" or "touches" rather than "observes." Tell children that they will be working like scientists to learn lots more about crayons.

What to look for

Children should be aware of and excited about working like scientists to learn more about crayons. Children should be able to use a magnifying lens to find out more information and details during an observation.

Helpful hint

Some children are challenged by working in a large group situation and may be too shy to contribute. You can meet with small groups and individuals to help children understand that participating and contributing their ideas is an important expectation. You may need to help some children practice using the magnifying lens correctly.

Part 2: Exploration

What is the exploration phase?

The exploration phase enables children to construct personal meaning through sensory experiences with objects, people, events, or concepts.

During exploration, children

- observe and explore materials,
- collect information, and
- construct their own understandings and meanings from their experiences.

The teacher's role is to

- facilitate, support, and enhance exploration;
- ask open-ended questions;
- respect children's thinking and rule systems;
- allow for constructive error; and
- model ways to organize information from experiences.

Exploration 1:
A Closer Look at Crayons

Exploring with their senses of touch, smell, and sight, children begin to discover more about crayons.

Duration

1 large group session

Purpose

- explore and observe crayons using the senses
- describe the characteristics of different types of crayons

What You Need

- poster board or large piece of paper
- class picture book from **Awareness 2: Getting Curious About Crayons**
- paper
- magnifying lenses
- assortment of crayons, including crayons with distinctive colors, sizes, thicknesses, shapes, and scents

Getting Ready

Prepare a class chart as shown.

Spotlight Vocabulary

- observe
- characteristic
- size words (such as long, short, thick, thin)
- texture words (such as smooth, rough, hard, soft)
- color words (such as brown, tan, red, blue)

Example of class chart

Begin

1. Use the picture book created in **Awareness 2: Getting Curious About Crayons** to review what the children have already learned about crayons. Afterwards, place the book in the reading center so children can review it on their own.

2. Give everyone paper, magnifying lenses, and an assortment of crayons. Discuss which of our senses can help us find out more about crayons. Allow children time to explore the crayons with their senses. (Remind children not to put the crayons in their mouth for safety reasons. This, of course, rules out using the sense of taste.)

Continue

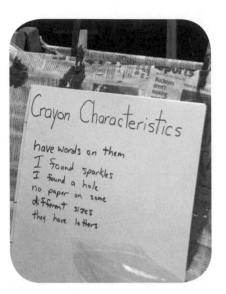

3. After the children have had time to explore their crayons with the appropriate senses, have them describe their observations. Record the characteristics the children describe on the class chart prepared in Getting Ready.

Questions to guide the observing process:
> *What do the crayons look like? Feel like? Smell like?*
> *What do you observe when you color with the crayons?*

Seen and heard:
   Children said, "They have different sizes," "It has words," "They feel greasy," and "I smell crayons."

4. Display the class chart so children and adults can review the results. The chart will also be used in **Exploration 2: Crayon Match Up** and **Exploration 3: Crayon Sorting**.

What to Look For

Encourage the children to use size, texture, color, and other detail words when describing their crayons. This exploration process should help children notice differences between crayons in future investigations.

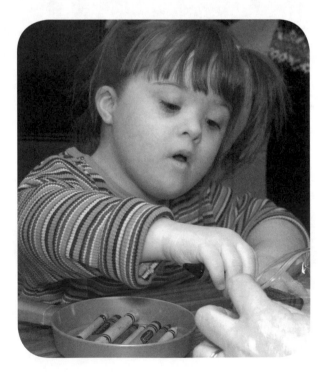

Exploration 2:
Crayon Match Up

Children take a closer look at their crayons as they try to find partners with matching crayons.

Duration

1 large group session, plus short daily sessions

Purpose

- compare crayon characteristics
- match pairs of crayons

What You Need

- assortment of crayons having distinct colors, sizes, wrappers, or other characteristics
- class chart from **Exploration 1: A Closer Look at Crayons**

Getting Ready

- Gather a set of crayons that can be paired as described in step 1 using color, size, and type of wrapper (different brands and wrapperless).
- Gather a second set of crayons so each child will have one crayon during step 2. Make sure multiple characteristics are available for pairing, such as color, size, and shape.

Spotlight Vocabulary

- match
- comparing words (such as same/different, bigger/smaller, thinner/thicker)

Begin

1. With the class, model how to match crayons into pairs based on different characteristics. For example, first match crayons into pairs based on color. Next, ask children to help you match pairs based on size. Lastly, have the children match pairs based on type of wrapper (different brands and wrapperless). Be sure to use many different comparing words when matching the crayons into pairs.

2. Let each child select a crayon from the second set of crayons prepared in Getting Ready. Do not mention the idea that there are pairs of matching crayons in the class. Help children build on the observations they made in **Exploration 1: A Closer Look at Crayons** by identifying the similarities and differences between the crayons.

Questions to guide the observing and comparing processes:

> *What do you notice about your crayon? Use your senses to observe your crayon. Describe what you observe.*

> *Which crayons are longer/shorter, thinner/fatter, and with wrappers/without wrappers?*

Seen and heard:

> Children said, "My crayon is blue," "It has no paper," and "It's flat on one side and curvy on the other side."

Continue

3. Ask the children to stand next to someone in the class who has a matching crayon. Children may find they have more than one partner. (No matter what criteria you had in mind for the matching pairs, be open to the criteria the children use.)

Questions to guide the organizing process:

> *Whose crayon is the same color as your crayon?*
> *Whose crayon is the same shape as your crayon?*
> *Whose crayon smells the same as your crayon?*

4. Have partners share their matching crayons with the class by explaining why they match. Encourage children to use words to describe the characteristics of the crayons. Discourage partners from using opinion words, such as prettiness and niceness, to describe their crayons. Scientists concentrate on facts rather than opinions. Add information to the class chart started during **Exploration 1: A Closer Look at Crayons** as partners identify features and characteristics that helped them match their crayons.

Questions to guide the comparing process:

> *How are your crayons alike?*
> *Why does your crayon match his crayon?*
> *How are your crayons different?*

Seen and heard:

> Children said, "Our crayons are sparkly," "They both have the same color," and "They are big."

5. On subsequent days, put an assortment of matching crayons in the science center for free exploration or small group sessions. Children should continue matching up crayons by examining different characteristics (such as color, length, shininess, and thickness).

What to Look For

Encourage partners to give an observable characteristic that explains their matching decision. Children may match with a partner based on a single characteristic. For example, a child with a yellow, round crayon may decide she has a match with a child holding a yellow, flat crayon. She could also have matched with a round crayon of a different color. No matter what characteristic you may have intended for children to use as a criteria for matching, be open to the possibility that children will use unexpected criteria. The objective of this activity is for children to have a reason for the match based on any characteristic they can observe and explain.

Have More Fun

❑ Show the children other types of writing tools that have similar characteristics to crayons and ask the children what characteristics the pairs of objects have in common. For example, show the children a yellow-colored pencil that matches the length of a purple crayon, a red pen that matches the color of a red crayon, and a big blue piece of sidewalk chalk that matches the shape of a thick orange crayon. Ask children to explain the features (such as length, color, or shape) that are common to the crayons and the other writing tools.

❑ Feature a "crayon of the day" that has a unique characteristic (for example, a metallic silver color). Throughout the day, ask children to locate other crayons and objects that have the same characteristic (for example, chair legs and sink faucets).

Exploration 3:
Crayon Sorting

Children take their exploration a step further by sorting sets of crayons into smaller groups.

Duration

1 large group session, 1 small group session, plus short daily sessions

Purpose

- compare crayon characteristics
- group crayons having similar characteristics
- discuss characteristics of crayons
- communicate crayon sorting through pictures and words

What You Need

- assortment of crayons varying in color, size, shape, and other characteristics
- ☞ *Select an appropriate number of crayons for the children to use in this sorting exercise. Younger children usually have more success working with a smaller selection of widely differing crayons. Children with more sorting experience can use a greater variety of crayons with more subtle differences.*
- class chart from **Exploration 1: A Closer Look at Crayons**

Spotlight Vocabulary

- sort
- observe
- group
- compare

Begin

Helpful Hint

This activity uses the class chart started in **Exploration 1: A Closer Look at Crayons** that lists children's descriptive words for crayon characteristics. If you did not do this activity, take time now to start a similar list.

1. Explain what "sort" and "group" mean by doing some examples with the class. Begin by telling the class you want to sort them into two groups. Ask the girls to go to one side of the room and the boys to go to the other.

Children were sorted into groups: those wearing jeans and those wearing other kinds of pants.

2. Gather the class together again. Tell them that now you want to sort the class based on type of shirt. For example, ask the class to split into those wearing striped shirts and those wearing shirts without stripes.

3. Have the class gather together again. Without the children knowing the criteria of your grouping, divide the class into three or more groups based on something else they are wearing (for example, long pants, short pants, and skirts/dresses). See if the class can guess why you grouped them the way that you did.

Continue

4. Gather together a small group of children and read the class chart of crayon characteristics started by the class during **Exploration 1: A Closer Look at Crayons**.

5. Place a collection of crayons where children can observe them. Tell the children to put together all the crayons they think belong together. Facilitate the children's efforts to place crayons into groups by listening to and commenting on the children's observations.

   Questions to guide the comparing and sorting processes:
   > *How are these crayons the same and how are they different?*
   > *Which ones could go together in a group?*
   > *Why did you group those crayons together?*

> ### Process Skill Power
>
> "Comparing is a powerful process that can lead to the understanding of many important scientific ideas."
>
> "Organizing is the process of putting objects or phenomena together on the basis of a logical rationale."
>
> Lawrence Lowery, 1992

Crayons have many characteristics (such as size, shape, with or without wrapper, and even scent) that enable a visually impaired child to participate in sorting.

Seen and heard:

> *Children said, "They have yellow," "The wrappers match," and "These roll."*

6. Once children have sorted the crayons into groups, ask them to point to each crayon group and explain the logic behind their sorting.

Questions to guide the communication process:

> *What can you say about how you sorted your crayons?*

> *Why did you put these crayons in this group?*

Seen and Heard:

> *Children said, "They look the same color brown" and "They have the same size."*

7. Have children record their sorting ideas by drawing pictures. As an alternative, take a picture of their sorted groups. Children can dictate their ideas to you so you can add captions.

8. On subsequent days, allow children to sort different collections of crayons either by working in small groups or individually.

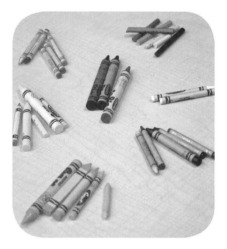

What to Look For

Be sure to let the children organize the crayons using their own classification systems; this will show you where they are in the development of sorting skills. Offer more opportunities to sort as the children continue to explore crayons. Children can show you what they are learning and will become more comfortable as they practice. Take notes and check their continuing development of this concept during the unit.

Younger children will generally create groups of items that are each based on a single property. Grouping items together (classifying) based on more than one characteristic is a more advanced skill that usually does not begin independently and consistently until age 7 or 8.

As you observe children exploring, take note of the various methods they use to learn more about crayons. Do they ask their friends questions? What do they notice while exploring with the materials? Are they able to use several senses to gather information? Your observations will help you discuss with children what they've learned.

Exploration 4:
Sharing Home Samples

Children bring their experiences with crayons into a new context by extending the fun of exploration and observation to their home.

Duration

1 large group session

Purpose

• look for and identify crayons at home
• communicate about crayons in front of the class

What You Need

• letter to parents (A sample is provided in this activity.)
• crayon samples and a drawn picture from home

Begin

1. Ask children to search for crayons at home, choose one, draw a picture of it, and bring the drawing and the crayon to share with the class. Provide children with a letter to families explaining the project or have children help you write the letter. (See the sample letter provided at the end of this activity.) Be aware that all children may not have crayons at home. However, they should still hunt for crayons to see what they find. Finding no crayons is information that can be recorded!

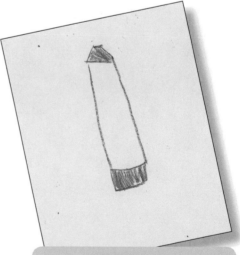

Continue

2. After the children bring in their pictures and crayons from home, gather the children into a large group to share their work. Before asking children to share, review what kinds of things they could tell the class about their crayons. It may be helpful if you bring a crayon

Helpful Hint

Allow children who didn't bring their work from home to choose a crayon from the class collection to draw and share.

from home as well. Children can help you tell about your crayon, then they will be ready to tell about theirs.

Questions to guide the communication process:

> *What can you share about your crayon?*

> *What is interesting about your crayon?*

> *Where did you find it?*

> *Why did you choose it?*

Seen and heard:

Children said, "My crayon is red," "It was in a drawer," and "It's my favorite."

3. Help children listen to other children's ideas. Depending upon the age and attention span of the children, you may choose to break the sharing time into shorter sessions.

4. Display the crayons and the pictures children brought to share. Encourage the children to visit the display to learn more about other children's work. Model for the class by visiting the display yourself and pointing out several things you learn by looking at the pictures and crayons.

Helpful Hint

Hang a clothesline high across the room or along one wall. Pictures and crayons can be attached to the clothesline with spring-type clothespins.

What to Look For

As you listen to details about the crayons that children share with one another, encourage them to include key crayon characteristics.

Dear Parents:

As part of our science explorations, we are studying about crayons. We've already looked at different kinds of crayons in our classroom, but now we would like to know more about the kinds of crayons we all have at home.

Please join your child in a search for crayons at home. There are many kinds of crayons. Hunt carefully and collect them to examine and compare. Once you have finished hunting for crayons, encourage your child to observe the crayons and tell you something about what he or she observes. You might want to assist in this observation by asking several questions: What does this crayon look like? What does it feel like? What kind of crayon is it? How big is it?

Have your child choose one crayon and draw a picture of it. Help them put their name on the paper because he or she will bring the picture to school to share with us. If your family doesn't have crayons at home—tell us that on the paper.

Also if possible, please allow your child to bring this chosen crayon to school to show the class. You can put it in a plastic bag with your child's name.

We will be sharing our home pictures and crayons in class on: _____.
Please help your child to remember to bring his or her work to school by _____. Thank you for your help. Have fun!

Sincerely,

Stop and Reflect

Review with the children what they have discovered so far about crayons using the class charts from previous activities for reference. Ask the children to share additional discoveries. You may wish to add ideas to the same charts or start a new chart summarizing their discoveries so far.

Guide the reflection process by asking

- What do you know about crayons now?
- What is interesting about crayons?
- What else would you like to know about crayons?
- How could we find out more?

Tell the children that they will be finding out more about crayons as scientists would do—by doing experiments with different crayons and the materials that make them. To include the children in the inquiry process, ask the class what they would like to know about crayons and how they could find answers. Children can surprise you with great ideas that are different than your plans. You may be able to incorporate their ideas into activities during the next phase of the learning cycle, the inquiry phase. There may be some questions that can't be answered easily—or sometimes not at all. That's okay. Scientists don't know everything and neither do we. On the other hand, we might be able to find out more in the future!

What to look for

All children can contribute something to explain what they have discovered during the unit so far. Some may need to refer to materials or samples of their work for ideas.

Part 3: Inquiry

What is the inquiry phase?

The inquiry phase of the learning cycle enables children to deepen and refine their understanding.

During inquiry, children

- examine,

- investigate,

- propose explanations,

- compare own thinking with that of others,

- generalize, and

- relate to prior learning.

The teacher's role is to

- help children refine understanding,

- ask more focused questions,

- provide information when requested, and

- help children make connections between prior experiences and their current investigations.

Inquiry 1:
Wax Tracks

Children look more closely at crayons and discover that crayon wax transfers to the object being colored.

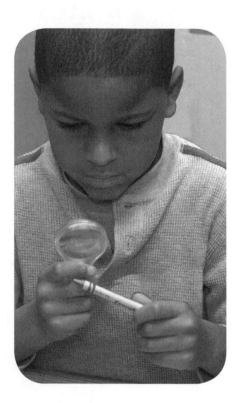

Duration

1 large group session

Purpose
- review that crayons are made from wax
- discover that wax comes off the crayon during coloring
- observe that small pieces of wax transfer to the paper during coloring

What You Need
- poster board or large piece of paper
- new (never used) crayons
- magnifying lenses
- paper

Getting Ready

Prepare the class chart as shown below.

Spotlight Vocabulary
- wax
- magnifying lens

Example of class chart

Before Coloring | After Coloring

Begin

1. Review the different types of crayons and the ways that the children sorted crayons in previous activities. Show children the book you read in **Awareness 3: The Crayon-Making Process** and review that crayons are made of wax.

   Question to guide interest:
   > *What is used to make crayons?*

   Seen and heard:
   > *Children said, "Wax!," "I helped my daddy wax the car," and "Hey, I've got wax in my ears!"*

2. Give each child a new crayon and a magnifying lens. Ask the children to use their eyes and magnifying lenses to look closely at the crayon's point and observe its shape. Draw the shape of a new crayon on the class chart (prepared in Getting Ready).

Continue

3. Have each child draw and color something on a piece of paper with their new crayon.

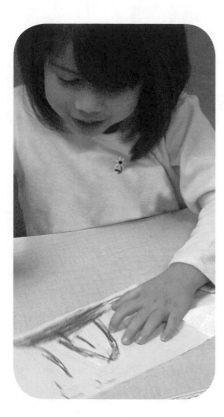

4. Ask the children to use their eyes and magnifying lenses to observe the points of their crayons now. Ask the children to describe their crayon points. Draw the shape of a used crayon on the class chart.

Question to guide interest:

> *How did the crayon point change when you colored?*

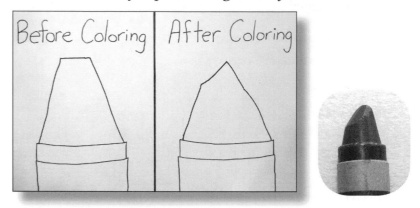

5. Ask the children to use their eyes, magnifying lenses, and fingers to observe the colored areas of their papers. Ask the children what happens to the crayon and to the paper when they color.

Questions to guide interest:

> *How did the paper change when you colored?*
> *Where does the color on the paper come from?*

Seen and heard:

> *Children said, "Wax goes on the paper" and "I feel wax."*

6. Explain to the children that pushing the crayon down on the paper makes wax come off the crayon and stick to the paper. Instruct the children to draw on their papers softly and notice that the lines are light. Now ask them to press hard with their crayons. Notice the lines are darker because more wax is forced off the crayon.

What to Look For

After coloring with their new crayons, look for children to notice that their crayon points have flattened and changed shape. Some children may figure out that the wax from the crayon went onto the paper. Help children understand that the more they color with their crayons, the more wax goes onto their paper.

Wax goes on the paper.

Student drawing about wax transferring to the paper from **Crayons Across the Curriculum 1: Writing to Learn.**

Inquiry 2:
Paper, Paper Everywhere

Children investigate how well crayons color on different types of paper. Children share ideas and observations with a partner and then with the class.

Helpful Hint

Inquiry 2: Paper, Paper Everywhere and **Inquiry 3: Try Coloring** are similar activities. Do both activities when children will benefit from reinforcement. Combine the two activities into one when reinforcement is not needed.

Duration

2 large group sessions, 1 small group session, and independent exploration

Purpose

- observe how crayons interact with different papers
- communicate observations to others

What You Need

- poster board or large piece of paper
- crayons
- small samples of corrugated cardboard and various other types of paper, such as newspaper, facial tissue, construction paper, and vellum
- 👉 *Younger children work better with a smaller selection of materials.*
- magnifying lenses
- (optional) test boards prepared in Getting Ready

Getting Ready

- Cut various papers into squares. If you want to make test boards, cut the materials into strips and tape the strips to light-weight cardboard. (See photo at top right.) Label as shown.
- Prepare a class chart on poster board or a large piece of paper by attaching samples of the materials as shown at bottom right.

Spotlight Vocabulary

- observe
- compare
- record
- material
- texture

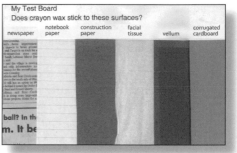

Example of test board

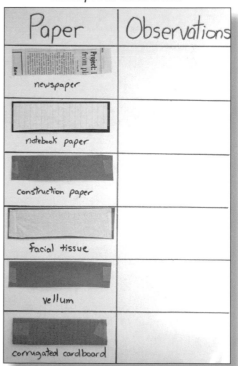

Example of class chart

Begin

Helpful Hint

When doing hands-on activities with the children, try to use "I wonder…" statements often to reinforce the way scientists think. Modeling the use of "I wonder…" throughout the unit should make **Advanced Inquiry 2: I Wonder…** easier for the children to do.

Helpful Hint

You may need to give children clues about how to work in pairs. Watch for successful pairs and share their strategies with the class. Do the partners take turns sharing ideas? How do the partners help each other? How do the partners offer their ideas to each other? How do the partners share materials?

1. Review the fact that crayons are made of wax and that coloring with crayons causes the wax to rub off the crayon and stick to the object being colored. Tell the children that you wonder if crayons will color on different kinds of paper. Show children the class chart (prepared in Getting Ready) and discuss what materials you want them to try coloring.

2. Have the children work in pairs. (Working with partners will encourage children to talk about their experiment and share ideas.) Give each person either squares of test materials or a test board you prepared in Getting Ready. Ask each child to color on the different paper using the same crayon. (You may want to give one partner a light-colored crayon and one a dark-colored crayon.)

3. As children are working, encourage them to observe their coloring carefully and talk with their partners about what they observe. They may touch the coloring and the paper. Have them listen while they color and use magnifying lenses for closer observation. (Pressing hard while coloring on the corrugated cardboard should cause a sound as the crayon rubs across the ridges.) Circulate and help the children focus on their work with questions.

Helpful Hint

Test materials should be saved for use in **Inquiry 4: Removing Crayon Marks.**

> *What do you notice about coloring on different paper?*

> *What do you hear and see?*

> *How do your results compare to your partner's results? What is the same? What is different?*

Seen and heard:

> *Children said, "It works" and "The cardboard is noisy."*

Continue

4. Gather the class together to discuss their observations. Encourage the children to look at their test materials and explain what they noticed. Record their observations on the class chart.

   Questions to facilitate the discussion:

   > *What do you notice about coloring on different paper?*

   > *Does the crayon wax stick to all kinds of paper?*

   > *Which papers were hardest to color?…easiest to color?*

5. Give the children additional time for free exploration. For example, put samples of the same and different types of paper in the science center with different types of crayons. The children may have new ideas to explore.

6. Display the class chart so children and adults can review the results.

What to Look For

Observe how children work cooperatively and collaboratively during this activity. These skills help children focus on and extend their discoveries. Listen for children to notice ways that the paper changes with color. Encourage children to observe how wax sticks to materials having different textures. Children should notice the sound made when coloring across the ridges of corrugated cardboard. Crayons can color on many different materials, but seem to color more easily on textured materials (such as construction paper and newspaper) than on smooth materials (such as vellum).

Inquiry 3:
Try Coloring

Children investigate how well crayons color on different materials. Children share ideas and observations with a partner and then with the class.

Example of test board

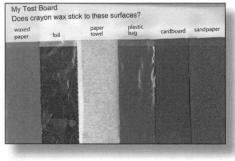

Example of class chart

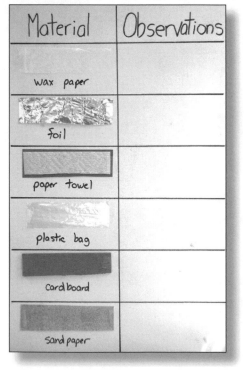

Duration

2 large group sessions, 1 small group session, and independent exploration

Purpose

- observe how crayons interact with different materials
- communicate observations to others

What You Need

- poster board or large piece of paper
- crayons
- small samples of various types of paper, plastic, and metal (such as wax paper, paper towel, cardboard, plastic sandwich bag, and foil)

☞ *Younger children work better with a smaller selection of materials.*

- magnifying lenses
- (optional) test boards prepared in Getting Ready

Getting Ready

- Cut various materials into squares. If you want to make test boards, cut the materials into strips and tape the strips to light-weight cardboard. (See photo at top left.) Label as shown.
- Prepare a class chart on poster board or a large piece of paper by attaching samples of the materials as shown at bottom left.

Spotlight Vocabulary

- observe
- compare
- record
- material
- texture

Begin

1. Review the fact that crayons are made of wax and that coloring with crayons causes the wax to rub off the crayon and stick to the object being colored. Tell the children that you wonder if crayons will color on different kinds of papers, plastics, and metals. Show children the class chart (prepared in Getting Ready) and discuss what materials you want them to try coloring.

2. Have the children work in pairs. (Working with partners will encourage children to talk about their experiment and share ideas.) Give each person either squares of test materials or a test board you prepared in Getting Ready. Ask each child to color on the materials using the same crayon. (You may want to give one partner a light-colored crayon and one a dark-colored crayon.)

3. As children are working, encourage them to observe their coloring carefully and talk with their partners about what they observe. They may touch the coloring and the materials. Have them use magnifying lenses for closer observation. Circulate and help the children focus on their work with questions.

   ### Questions to facilitate the processes of observing:
   > *What do you notice about coloring on different materials?*
   > *Which materials are hard to color on? Why?*
   > *How do your results compare to your partner's results? What is the same? What is different?*

   ### Seen and heard:
   Children said, "It colors on everything," "It won't color on wax paper or plastic," and "Wax got onto the foil."

Continue

4. Gather the class together to discuss their observations. Encourage the children to look at their test materials and explain what they noticed. Record their observations on the class chart.

Children noticed small flakes of wax coming off the crayons.

Helpful Hint

Test materials should be saved for use in **Inquiry 4: Removing Crayon Marks.**

Questions to facilitate the discussion:
> *What do you notice about coloring on different materials?*
> *Which materials are hard to color on? Why?*
> *Does the crayon wax stick to all the materials?*

5. Give the children additional time for free exploration. For example, put samples of the same and different test materials in the science center with different types of crayons. The children may have new ideas to explore.

6. Display the class chart so children and adults can review the results.

What to Look For

Observe how children work cooperatively and collaboratively during this activity. These skills help children focus on and extend their discoveries. Listen for children to notice ways that the materials change with color. Encourage children to observe how wax sticks to materials having different textures. Crayons can color on many different materials, but seem to color more easily on textured materials (such as paper towel and newspaper) than on smooth materials (such as plastic sandwich bags and wax paper).

Have More Fun

❑ Give the children a chance to color on things they normally aren't allowed to color. Gather a selection of objects such as a metal clipboard, pieces of wood (painted and unpainted), empty milk containers (plastic jug and paper carton), and rocks (smooth and rough). Put these materials in the science center with different types of crayons. After free exploration, discuss and record class observations.

Inquiry 4:
Removing Crayon Marks

Children explore ways to remove crayon wax from different materials and observe their results. Can crayon marks be removed or are they permanent?

Duration

2 large group sessions and 1 small group session

Purpose

- observe and compare different ways to remove crayon wax
- observe and compare how different removal methods affect the crayon marks and the materials
- record and share ideas

What You Need

- poster board or large piece of paper
- tape
- small pieces of paper
- pencils with erasers
- assortment of crayons
- test materials children colored during **Inquiry 2: Paper, Paper Everywhere** and **Inquiry 3: Try Coloring**
- objects to remove crayon marks such as pencil erasers, plastic spoons, wooden craft sticks, paper towels, facial tissues, dry sponges, and pot scrubbers
- magnifying lenses

Be Safe

Do not let children try cleaning products other than those listed in "What You Need."

Getting Ready

- Experiment with various materials and removal techniques so you can discover results and ask the children more relevant questions.

Example of class chart

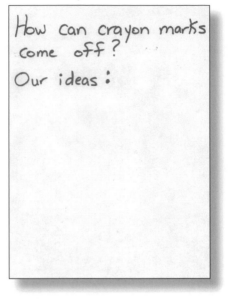

How can crayon marks come off?
Our ideas:

• Prepare two class charts as shown. Tape examples of the removal objects and all the test materials to the second chart (shown below) so nonreaders can follow along.

Example of class chart

Which tools remove crayon marks from these materials?

newspaper
foil
plastic bag
cardboard
paper towel
wax paper

Spotlight Vocabulary

• words to describe changes in pattern and color (such as lighter, darker, fading, disappearing, smearing, blurry)

• words to describe small pieces or marks (such as specks, dots, flecks, spots)

Begin

1. Review with the class that crayons can color on a lot of different materials. Show the class some of the materials they colored in **Inquiry 2: Paper, Paper Everywhere** and **Inquiry 3: Try Coloring**. Tell the class that now you wonder how crayon marks can be taken *off* different materials.

2. Give each child a small piece of paper, a pencil with an eraser, and a crayon. Have the children draw a line with the pencil. Ask how they can take the pencil mark off the paper. After the idea of erasing comes up, ask children to try it.

3. Have each child draw a line with the crayon. Ask how they can take the crayon mark off the paper. After the idea of erasing comes up, ask children to try it. Point out that the crayon mark smears and does not come off like the pencil mark does.

4. Ask the children to come up with ways of getting crayon marks off different materials. Record their ideas on the first class chart prepared in Getting Ready. You may have to ask questions to spark ideas.

    Questions to guide the discussion:
    > *What are some ways people clean in their homes?*
    > *What do people use to get mud off shoes?*
    > *What are some ways to clean dishes?*

5. After the children share their ideas, show them things that you were thinking might remove crayon marks. Discuss the second class chart you prepared in Getting Ready, which shows the test materials and the removal techniques the children are going to try. You can add additional removal techniques based on the children's ideas.

Continue

6. Have children work in pairs to test the removal methods on the papers colored during **Inquiry 2: Paper, Paper Everywhere** and **Inquiry 3: Try Coloring**. Have children use magnifying lenses to more closely observe the results. As children are working, circulate and help them focus on their work with questions.

    Questions to guide the observing and comparing process:
    > *How well does the eraser remove crayon marks? Describe what happens to the crayon marks, the material, and the eraser.*
    > *How well does scraping remove crayon marks? Describe what happens to the crayon marks, the material, and the scraper.*
    > *How well does wiping remove crayon marks? Describe what happens to the crayon marks, the material, and the wiper.*

    Seen and heard:
    > Children said, "It doesn't come off," "The color rubs around," and "Wax comes off on the paper towel."

7. Gather the class together with their test materials to discuss their observations. Ask each pair of children to discuss one way they tried to remove crayon marks, including what happened when they tried that method. Record results on the appropriate class chart by drawing lines from the removal technique to the materials from which the crayon was successfully removed. You may have to demonstrate removal methods that the children don't remember. Also, be sure to show that objects such as erasers and paper towels gather crayon wax during the removal process. Summarize the results with the class.

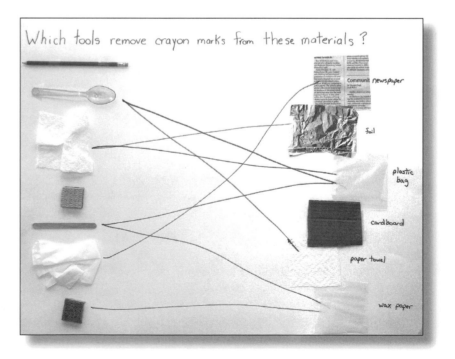

Questions to facilitate the comparison of methods:

> *Which method worked the best? Why?*

> *Does it matter what kind of crayon pattern you try to remove? Circles? Lines? Scribbles?*

> *Which material was the hardest to clean? Why?*

> *What problems came up while you were trying to remove crayon marks?*

8. Display the class charts so children and adults can review the results.

What to Look For

Look for children to actively explore the removal methods and work cooperatively with their partners. Some children may notice finer details than other children. For example, some children may notice that erasers and dry sponges smear and blur the crayon marks. Some children may notice that craft sticks and plastic spoons scrape off bits of crayon wax. Be sure to point out that some removal objects (such as erasers and paper towels) collect crayon wax while removing wax from the materials. Help the children explain their observations. Finally, ask children "Why do we *not* color on the walls or furniture with crayons?"

*Student drawing about removing crayon wax from paper from **Crayons Across the Curriculum 1: Writing to Learn.***

Inquiry 5:
Wax and Water

Children examine the water resistance of wax paper, crayon wax, and marks made by other drawing tools.

Duration

1 small group session

Purpose

- observe that water beads up on wax paper and crayon wax
- observe the interactions of crayon wax with water and watercolor paints
- compare the interactions of watercolor paints with crayon, colored pencil, and permanent marker drawings

What You Need

- permanent marker (for teacher use only)
- paper durable enough for use with watercolor paints
- paper towel
- eyedropper, straw, or disposable pipette
- wax paper
- colored pencils
- crayons
- watercolor supplies (watercolor paint, brushes, and cups of water)

Getting Ready

- Cut paper towel and wax paper into small pieces so each child will get one of each type of material.
- Prepare a test paper for each child by drawing three different shapes as shown. Color one of the shapes with permanent marker. Children will color the other shapes in step 3.

Spotlight Vocabulary

- absorb
- beads up
- wax
- coat (to cover something)
- waterproof
- watercolor paint
- shape words (such as circle, triangle, square)

Example of test paper

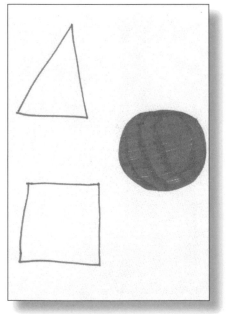

Begin

1. Give each child a small piece of paper towel. Use an eyedropper, straw, or disposable pipette to place a drop of water on each paper towel. Ask the children what happens to the water. (Point out that the water is absorbed, or soaked up, by the paper towel.)

    Seen and heard:

    Children said, "The water sunk in" and "It's soaking up the water."

2. Next, give each child a small piece of wax paper. Place a drop of water on the wax paper. Ask the children what happens to the water. (Point out that the water beads up and rolls around the paper. The wax coating does not absorb the water because the wax coating is waterproof.)

    Seen and heard:

    Children said, "It's moving around," "It slid off," and "It looks like a roly-poly!"

3. Give each child the test paper with three drawn shapes you prepared in Getting Ready. One of the shapes will already be colored with permanent marker. Ask the children to color one of the other shapes with colored pencil and the remaining shape with crayon. Be sure they heavily fill in the shapes with color.

4. Review the fact that coloring with crayon covers the area with wax. Ask the children what they think will happen when water is dropped on each test paper shape. After children respond, test and see. The water should bead up on the crayon shape like it did on the wax paper (since both are coated with wax). The water should spread out on the other shapes similar to the way it spreads on the paper towel.

Continue

5. Distribute watercolor supplies and ask the children to paint with watercolors over the shapes. Ask them to observe and discuss what happens.

Questions to guide the observations and comparisons:

> How has the watercolor paint changed the paper?

> What do you notice about the watercolor paint on each shape?

> Which coloring materials are waterproof?

Seen and heard:

Children said, "The triangle is getting wet" and "I colored my box blue and the water didn't stick."

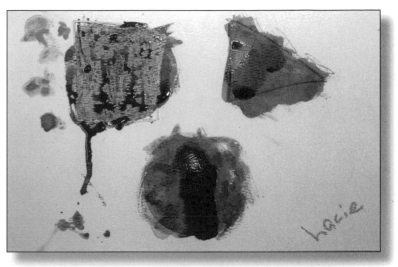

The square coated with crayon wax is waterproof.

What to Look For

During step 4, look for children to relate the wax coating on wax paper to the crayon wax coating they color on their papers. Some children may need extra help with understanding this correlation. Children should observe that only the crayon-colored shape on their test paper is waterproof.

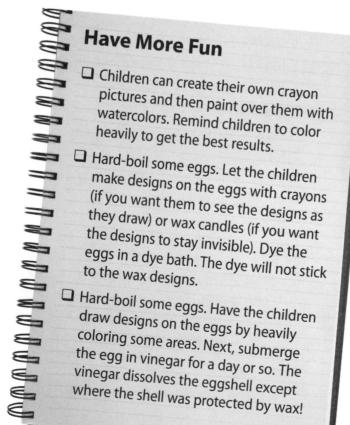

Have More Fun

❑ Children can create their own crayon pictures and then paint over them with watercolors. Remind children to color heavily to get the best results.

❑ Hard-boil some eggs. Let the children make designs on the eggs with crayons (if you want them to see the designs as they draw) or wax candles (if you want the designs to stay invisible). Dye the eggs in a dye bath. The dye will not stick to the wax designs.

❑ Hard-boil some eggs. Have the children draw designs on the eggs by heavily coloring some areas. Next, submerge the egg in vinegar for a day or so. The vinegar dissolves the eggshell except where the shell was protected by wax!

Inquiry 6:
Major Meltdown

Children discover that heat melts crayons, changing them from *solid* to *liquid*. As liquid crayons cool, they become *solid* again.

Duration

1 large group session and 1 small group session

Purpose

- explore a phase change
- observe crayons before, during, and after melting and after cooling

What You Need

- poster board or large piece of paper
- index cards
- 3 clear plastic cups
- two ice cubes
- assortment of crayons

☞ *Crayola® crayons melt more easily than other brands. Thin crayons are easier to break into fourths.*

- paper or foil cupcake liners (muffin cups)
- hair dryer (for teacher use only)
- paper for children to record (draw) their observations
- rectangular pieces of wax paper
- tape
- permanent marker (for teacher use only)
- crayon sharpener
- (optional) craft stick

Example of class chart

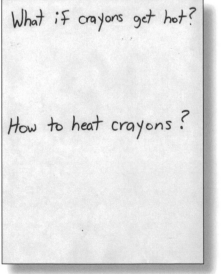

Be Safe

Keep the hair dryer and hot wax away from children and high traffic areas. Be careful with the electrical cord. Remind children to stay away from hot appliances.

Getting Ready

- Prepare a class chart as shown at left.
- Prepare index cards as shown at right.

Example of index cards

- Test the hair dryer to determine how much time and heat you need to do the melting in steps 4 and 9. Also plan for the best way to keep your children safe.

- Peel the labels off the crayons you plan to use in this activity. The labels come off more easily if the crayons are soaked in water.

- Rather than have children record their steps 3, 4, and 5 observations on blank paper, you can prepare a data sheet for each child as shown at bottom right. The lines at the top of each column are to record "solid" or "liquid."

- To save time in step 7, make crayon shavings ahead of time by scraping the sides of wrapperless crayons with a craft stick or sharpening crayons to collect the pieces.

- Right before doing step 1, put a small amount of water in one cup, an ice cube in a second cup, and a small amount of water and an ice cube in a third cup.

Spotlight Vocabulary

- melt
- liquid
- wax paper
- solid
- harden
- words to describe small pieces (such as specks, dots, flecks, spots)
- temperature words (such as hot, warm, cool)

Example of data sheet

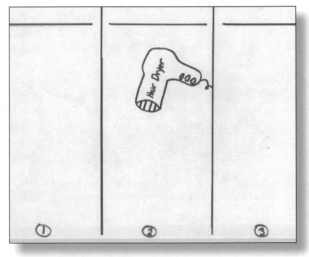

Begin

1. Show children the cup of water and ask if water is solid or liquid. Ask them to name other liquids. Hold up the index card representing liquid. Show children the cup containing the ice cube and ask if ice is solid or liquid. Ask them to name other solids. Hold up the index card representing solid. Show children the cup containing the water and an ice cube. Ask them what is happening to the ice cube.

Seen and heard:

When holding up the first cup, children said "Water is liquid" and the other liquids include "soup," "oil," "milk," and "juice." When holding up the second cup, children said "Ice is solid" and other solids include "bricks," "frozen strawberries," and "sticks." When holding up the third cup, a child said "The ice is melting and is a liquid now."

2. Tell children that you wonder what would happen if crayons got hot. Ask children for their ideas. Also ask how crayons could be heated. Record their thoughts on the class chart prepared in Getting Ready.

Questions to guide interest:
> *What would happen to a crayon if it got hot?*
> *How can we heat the crayon to find out?*

Seen and heard:
> *Children said, "It will burn," "They will melt," and "Put them in the oven."*

3. Break a crayon with no label into fourths. Put two pieces of the crayon in each of two cupcake liners. Ask children to draw the crayon pieces and record if they are solid or liquid. (Children can copy the words from the index cards.)

4. Use a hair dryer on the hottest setting to melt the crayon pieces in one of the cupcake liners. Let children observe what happens to the crayon from a safe distance. Tilt the cupcake liner slightly so the children can see that the crayon melts. (You don't have to melt the crayon entirely to demonstrate that the heat melts the crayon.) Ask the children what is happening. Tell children to draw what happens when the crayons are heated and record if the crayon pieces are solid or liquid.

Questions to guide the reflection process:
> *What do you notice about the pieces of crayon after heating them?*
> *How did the heat change the crayon pieces? Are they solid or liquid?*

Seen and heard:
> *Children said, "It's shiny," "It's wet," and "It's melting."*

Let's Sing

Solid, Liquid
(sung to the tune of Frère Jacques)

Solid, liquid

Solid, liquid

See crayons melt.

See crayons melt.

Heat the crayons to melt them.

Heat the crayons to melt them.

See crayons melt.

See crayons melt.

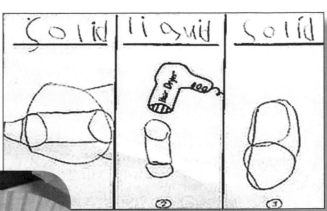

5. After the children have drawn and the melted crayon has cooled, take the solid crayon disk out of the cupcake liner. Let the children feel the wax and ask if it is solid or liquid. Have the children draw and record what they observe.

Questions to guide the reflection process:

> *What do you notice about the crayon now that it's not hot any more?*

> *How did the crayon change?*

Seen and heard:

Children said, "It's smooth," "It's frozen now," and "It's hard."

6. Ask the children if this crayon disk is the same now as it was before it was melted. Ask them how they can find out. Have children test their ideas with an original crayon piece and the crayon disk. After the tests, point out that the crayon material after melting is the same as it was before, except its shape is changed.

Helpful Hint

To test the crayon pieces and disk, children can color on different materials and test waterproof ability.

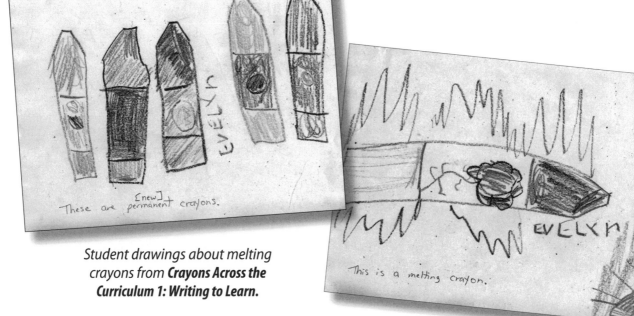

Student drawings about melting crayons from **Crayons Across the Curriculum 1: Writing to Learn.**

These are [new] permanent crayons.

This is a melting crayon.

Continue

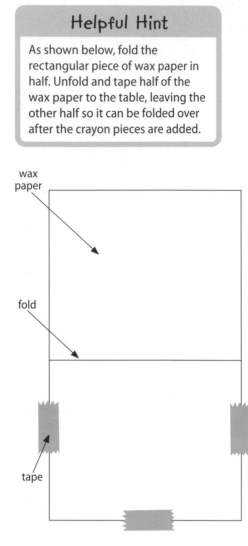

wax paper

fold

tape

7. Tape one rectangular piece of wax paper to the table for each child. (See Helpful Hint.) Add children's names to the wax paper with a permanent marker. Show a small group of children how to use a crayon sharpener to make crayon shavings. Collect the small pieces of crayon over the wax paper. If you prepared shavings in Getting Ready, children can add the shavings to their wax paper.

8. Ask the children what would happen if heat were added to the crayon pieces. Let the children reflect and predict what would happen based on what they have learned so far.

Questions to guide the reflection process:

> *If I use a hair dryer on the crayon pieces, what will happen?*
> *How will the pieces change?*
> *Why do we need to be careful with heat?*

Seen and heard:

Children said, "Melt" and "It would get hot."

9. Fold each piece of wax paper in half so the crayon pieces are covered. Tape all along the open edges of the wax paper to hold the flap down and prevent hot wax from leaking out. Use a hair dryer on the hottest setting to warm all areas of the wax paper. (Be sure children keep their hands away from the wax paper.) Children can watch the crayon melt, liquefy, and spread within the wax paper. When it is safe, let the children feel and observe the wax paper as the crayon hardens back into a solid. Ask the children what happened. Have children draw their observations.

Questions to guide the reflection process:

> *What do you notice about the pieces of crayon right after they have been heated with the hair dryer?*

> *What do you notice about the crayon wax when the paper isn't hot anymore?*

Seen and heard:

Children said, "It got mushy," "It's liquid," and "It's pretty."

What to Look For

Look for children to actively observe the changes in the crayons during each step of the procedure. Notice how the children document what they observe.

Have More Fun

☐ Place a wax paper "sandwich" filled with crayon pieces on top of brown paper. Place more brown paper on top and iron for about 10 seconds on medium heat. Let cool before allowing the children to observe the results.

☐ On a hot sunny day, seal a crayon in a zipper-type plastic bag. Put the bag on a tray and then on a car dashboard in full sun. If conditions are right, the wax will melt in the bag. This is a good way to remind children *not* to stay in a hot car! If possible, try this activity again on a cold sunny day.

Crayon in a bag after sitting on a car dashboard on a sunny day

Inquiry 7:

What Is a Crayon?

Children learn that objects can be made from different materials. For example, crayons are made from wax, powdered pigment (for the color), and paper (for the label). Children then extend their experiences by searching at home for things made of wax.

Duration

2 large group sessions

Purpose

- learn that writing tools are made from specific materials
- look for and identify wax at home
- communicate about wax

What You Need

- pencils
- materials that represent the parts of a pencil (such as wood, aluminum foil, large eraser, and mechanical pencil graphite)
- washable markers
- materials that represent the parts of a washable marker (such as plastic beads, felt, and colored water)
- crayons
- materials that represent the parts of a crayon (such as paraffin wax, powdered pigment, and paper)
- magnifying lenses
- wax objects placed in your classroom (such as wax paper, birthday candle, and milk or juice carton)

Spotlight Vocabulary

- material
- wax
- parts
- property

Begin

1. Lay out, in random order, all of the materials you gathered that represent parts of a pencil, washable marker, and crayon. Guide the children to identify each of the materials.

2. Show the children pencils. Ask them to observe the parts of the pencil and then pick out what materials are used to make a pencil. (See Helpful Hints.) Have children use magnifying lenses for a closer look. Help the children identify each material and its role in making the pencil work.

   ### *Questions to guide the observing:*
   > *What material makes the pencil point?*
   > *What does the pencil point do?*
   > *What material makes the pink end of the pencil?*
   > *What does the eraser do?*

   ### *Seen and heard:*
   Children said, "A pencil writes" and "Erasers take it off."

Helpful Hints

- Pencils are made from wood, metal, rubber or vinyl (the eraser), and graphite.
- Washable markers are made from plastic, cotton-like filament (that holds the ink), and colored ink.
- Crayons are made from wax, colored powder, and paper.

3. Tell the children that engineers are scientists. Engineers learn all about the properties of different materials, then decide what materials to use when creating and building something. Repeat step 2 with washable markers and then with crayons. (See Helpful Hints.) Be sure to ask children to observe the properties of the materials they are choosing.

4. Ask the children to help you search for wax in the classroom. Help them find objects such as wax paper, a birthday candle, and a small paper milk or juice carton. Explain that wax can be tricky to find— sometimes people use it and don't know it. Ask children to describe wax, including how it feels. Remind them what happened when they colored on paper and then dropped water on the wax. (Wax is waterproof.)

Seen and heard:

Children said, "Here is a candle," "I found that slippery paper," and "It feels oily."

5. Ask children to search for wax at home, choose one object made of wax, draw a picture of it, and bring the drawing (and ideally the object) to share with the class. Provide children with a letter to families explaining the project or have children help you write the letter. (See the sample letter provided at the end of this activity.) Be aware that all children may not have wax objects at home. However, they should still hunt for these objects to see what they find. Finding none of these objects is information that can be shared with the class!

Continue

6. After their home assignment is complete, gather the children into a large group to share their work as in steps 2–4 of **Exploration 4: Sharing Home Samples**.

   ### Questions to guide the communication process:
   > *What can you share about your object?*
   > *Where did it come from?*
   > *How did you find it?*
   > *How is your object used?*
   > *Why did you choose it?*

Helpful Hint

Allow children who didn't bring their work from home to choose a wax object from the class collection to draw and share.

What to Look For

Watch for children to notice key characteristics or properties of the materials used to make pencils, washable markers, and crayons. Look for details in observations and discussions that show critical thinking skills. Encourage children to apply their knowledge of wax during their home searches. Look for a wide variety of objects from home, since wax is included in many common objects in our lives today. (See the waxes section in Part 8: All About Crayons and Wax for a list of products containing wax.) As children share details about the wax they brought home, encourage them to include properties and characteristics of wax.

Dear Parents,

As part of our science explorations, we have been studying crayons in science. We've learned many things about crayons, including the fact that crayons are made from wax. We would like to know more about how people use different kinds of wax at home.

Please join your child in a search for wax in and around your home. Hunt carefully and collect objects and products containing wax to examine and compare. Once you have finished hunting for wax, encourage your child to observe the objects and tell you something about what he or she observes. You might want to assist in this observation by asking several questions. Where did you find the wax? What is it used for? What does it look like? If your child can explore your samples safely, take a small sample and feel it—or pour or rub it on a piece of paper. Is there a color? Is there a smell? How does it feel? Your child can bring these pieces of information back to share with the class—we love information!

Have your child choose one wax object or product and draw a picture of it. Help them to put their name on the paper and bring the picture to school to share with us. If your family doesn't have wax at home, tell us that on the paper.

Also, if possible, please allow your child to bring this object or product to school to show the class. You can put it in a plastic bag with your child's name.

We will be sharing our home wax and pictures in class on_____. Please help your child to remember to bring his or her work to school by _____. Thank you for your help. Have fun!

Sincerely,

Inquiry 8:
How Heavy Are Crayons?

Children investigate and compare the weights of various crayons and crayon combinations.

Duration
1 small group session, 1 large group session, and independent exploration

Purpose
- match the weights of crayons to counters serving as weights
- watch the balance to see when the weights on the two sides of the balance match
- count the number of counters that made the balance level
- compare the weights of various crayons

What You Need
- poster board or large piece of paper
- tape
- small, snack-sized plastic bags
- primary or bucket balances
- set of same-sized counters (such as plastic counting bears or centimeter/gram cubes)
- object (not a crayon) to weigh during demonstration
- assortment of different-sized crayons

Be Safe
Remind children to keep counters out of their mouth.

Getting Ready
- Create a class chart as shown. Tape plastic bags in the "crayons" column so children can display the crayons after weighing them.
- To save class time and better control the crayon combinations in step 2, you can place various groups of crayons in different plastic bags and seal the bags with tape. Children can select and weigh the bags they want to investigate, then tape the bags on the class chart.

Example of class chart

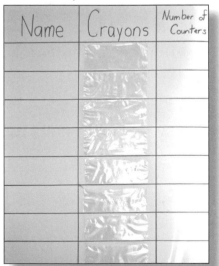

Spotlight Vocabulary

- heavy
- light
- counters
- weight
- balance
- objects
- measure
- comparison words (such as more, less, add, take away)

Begin

1. Demonstrate to a small group of children how to use a simple balance. Model how to use the counters by weighing an object that is not a crayon.

Questions to guide the observing and comparing processes:

> *What happens when I put the object in the balance pan? What does it mean?*

> *How do you know if the object on one side of the balance is heavier/lighter than the counters on the other side of the balance?*

> *How do you know if both balance pans have the same weight?*

Seen and heard:

Children said, "That one's up and that one's down," This side is heavier," and "The thing is flat now."

Helpful Hint

If children are not familiar with balances, giving them free exploration time prior to this activity will help the children focus better in step 3.

Continue

2. Tell the children that you wonder how much crayons weigh. Ask each child to select one crayon or a group of crayons to weigh. (You may have to establish a maximum allowable amount of crayons.) If you did not group the crayons ahead of time (see Getting Ready), encourage children to select different crayon combinations.

    ### *Seen and heard:*

    > *Children said, "I want the red one," "Give me the fat one and little one," and "I want the two big ones."*

3. Have children work in pairs so they can help each other. Ask each child to weigh his or her crayons by putting the crayons on one side of the balance and enough counters on the other side to make the balance level. Then, children should count the number of counters they used and record the results on the class chart. (You may need to help younger children fill out the chart.) The crayons that were weighed should go into the appropriate plastic bags on the chart.

    ### *Questions to guide the inquiry process:*

    > *> Did both pans balance?*
    > *> How many counters did you need to match the crayon's weight?*

    ### *Seen and heard:*

    > *Children said, "I put one in and it went down," "Should I take one out?," and "Mine weighs three."*

4. Once all the children have weighed their crayons and recorded their data, meet as a class. Ask each child to explain what they found out, then ask the class to compare and discuss the results.

5. Give children the opportunity to continue this investigation on their own.

   Questions to guide the investigation:
   > *What do you wonder about crayons and their weights?*
   > *How can you find out?*
   > *What did you do to find out?*
   > *What happened?*
   > *Do you wonder about anything else now?*

What to Look For

Look for the strategies that children use to organize their testing of materials. How do they keep track of how much each crayon or group of crayons weighs? How can they explain the differences between different crayons and different crayon combinations? Do the children work with materials in a random or methodical way? How persistent are they in finding out more about crayons? How many tests are they willing to try?

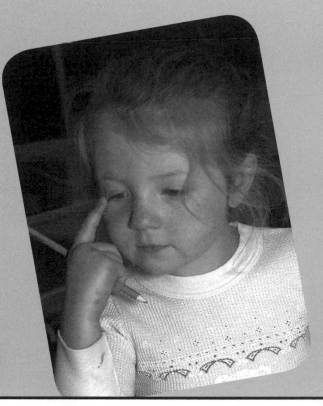

Stop and Reflect

Set up a display of the children's recorded observations. In small groups, meet with the children to view and discuss the display. Record their ideas and add them to the display for others to see. Read their ideas aloud and share them with the class.

Guide the discussion process by asking

- What do you think about your own work?
- What do you notice about crayons by looking at the group's work?
- What do you want to remember about crayons and wax?
- What was something new that you learned by doing these activities?
- What is important to remember about wax?

Part 4:
Advanced Inquiry

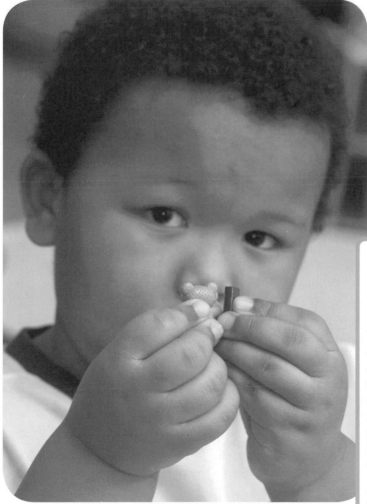

How are advanced inquiry activities different?

The first advanced inquiry activity expands early comparing and measuring skills to include estimating and using crayons as nonstandard units of measure. The second activity allows children to plan and test their own procedures based on what they wonder about crayons and wax.

Each activity in this section begins with teachers modeling the inquiry. Later steps allow children to continue the inquiry process on their own.

Advanced Inquiry 1:
Size It Up

Children practice comparing by matching the lengths of crayons to the lengths of other objects in the classroom.

Duration

1 large group session and independent exploration

Purpose

- find objects having the same length as various crayons
- share and record results
- build a foundation for measurement concepts and skills

What You Need

- assortment of crayons having different lengths (include some broken crayons)
- assortment of objects having lengths matching the lengths of various crayons

The objects you select can include index cards, pencils, craft sticks, and stacked centimeter/gram cubes.

- other objects in the classroom having lengths matching the lengths of various crayons
- graph paper

Getting Ready

- Gather the objects you will present to the class in step 1.

Spotlight Vocabulary

- match
- compare
- length
- same/different

Begin

1. Lay out, in random order, all the objects you gathered that have lengths matching those of various crayons. Guide the children to identify each of the objects.

2. Show the children a crayon. Tell them that you wonder if any of the gathered objects have the same length as the crayon. Put the crayon next to different objects to find an object that matches the length of the crayon. Ask the children to tell you when the lengths match.

   ### Questions to guide the observing and comparing processes:

   > *How can I tell if the length of this crayon matches the length of this object?*

   > *Do the lengths match?*

   ### Seen and heard:

   A child said, "The red one matches the pencil."

3. With help from the children, match the lengths of various other crayons to the lengths of various other objects. Make sure each child understands the process.

Continue

4. Divide the class into pairs and ask each pair to select a crayon. Tell the partners to search the classroom for an object that has a length matching their crayon. Try to let the partners search on their own, but help those who are having difficulty.

5. Give children graph paper and ask them to draw their crayons and their matching objects. Tell them to be sure to draw both objects the same length.

6. Gather the class together. Ask each pair of children to show the class their crayon, object, and drawings.

What to Look For

Look for children to understand the concept of matching lengths. Some children may need more practice than others. Listen for comments and questions that children ask each other as they work in pairs. Observe how children work cooperatively and collaboratively during this activity.

Have More Fun

☐ Give pairs of children empty crayon boxes or snack-size zipper-type plastic bags. (If crayon boxes are used, cut off or block out the crayon counts shown on the packages prior to the activity.) Ask children to estimate how many crayons will fit in their containers while still being able to close (or zip) the tops. You or the children should write down their estimates. After children fill the containers, have them count the crayons that fit and then compare these counts to their estimates. Partners can then share their results with the class. Repeat this activity as time permits because practice typically leads to more accurate estimating.

Advanced Inquiry 2:
I Wonder...

Children participate in discovery activities with crayons and wax.

Duration
2 large group sessions and 1 small group session

Purpose
- learn the process of discovery by asking questions, planning and doing investigations, and recording results
- communicate results to the class

What You Need
- poster board or large piece of paper
- class charts and children's work from previous activities
- materials determined by the children
- I Wonder Data Sheet provided at the end of this activity

Getting Ready
- Prepare a class chart as shown.
- Make copies of the I Wonder Data Sheet. Make extras in case some children need to start over.

Spotlight Vocabulary
- investigate
- experiment
- plan
- test
- wonder
- record

Example of class chart

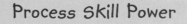

Class Chart

We wonder _____

What We Plan to Do

What We Found Out

Process Skill Power

"What separates true inquiry from play are the processes of observing and questioning, and then developing and following a plan of action."

Jane Bresnick, 2000

Begin

An Example

"I wonder if a crayon will melt in hot water."

Helpful Hint

Ask the children detailed questions during the planning stage, such as "How should we get the water hot? How hot should the water be? What should we put the water in? What type of crayon should we try? Should we take the paper off the crayon before dropping it in the hot water? Should we break the crayon?"

1. Gather the children together and ask them to share what they have learned about crayons and wax. Show the class charts and work from previous activities. Remind children about all the things you have wondered about and all the things that were found out. Explain that scientists are always looking for more to learn. Model the inquiry process by making an "I wonder" statement that is easily testable. (See example at left.)

2. Write down your "I wonder" statement on the class chart prepared in Getting Ready. Ask the children specific questions to come up with a plan for testing the "I wonder" statement. (See Helpful Hint at left.) Draw a picture depicting the plan in the "What We Plan to Do" section of the class chart. (See photo below.)

Questions to guide the inquiry:

> *How can we test what we are wondering about?*

> *What things do we need for our test?*

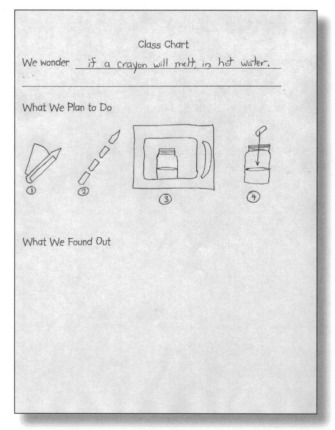

A class plan could be to take the paper off a regular-sized crayon, break the crayon into fourths, use a microwave to heat water to boiling in a clear mason jar, and drop one crayon piece into the jar of boiling water.

3. As a class, conduct the test outlined by the children. With the help of the children, complete the "What We Found Out" section of the class chart.

Continue

4. Working in small groups, ask the children what other things they wonder about crayons and wax. It may be helpful to review with the children the previous activities that they did. Describing previous procedures and results may help children think of things they still wonder about.

5. Ask the children in each small group to come up with one "I wonder" statement that relates to crayons and/or wax. Guide the children to discuss and agree upon one plan for testing their statement. Help the group fill out an I Wonder Data Sheet (prepared in Getting Ready) by drawing a procedure in the "What I Plan to Do" portion of the data sheet that represents what they are going to try. Older children may fill out their own data sheets.

Questions to guide the inquiry process:

> *What do you wonder about crayons or wax?*

> *How can you test your idea?*

> *What do you need to use for your test?*

Helpful Hints

Allow the children to come up with their own plan for testing the "I wonder" statement. The investigation process is more meaningful to children when they design and implement their own procedures rather than use procedures outlined by the teacher.

During the inquiry process, the teacher should observe, question, and support the efforts of the children. Some redirecting of the children's plan may be necessary. You may also have to assist some children who have a hard time articulating their ideas by helping them find the right words.

6. Have the children conduct their test, and then assist the group as needed in drawing and writing to complete the "What I Found Out" portion of the data sheet.

7. Gather the class together and ask each group of children to show their data sheets and describe their findings.

What to Look For

Mastering the inquiry learning process takes lots of time and practice. Some children may have difficulty with all or some of the questioning, planning, testing, and recording steps. Modeling the process and working with children in small groups will help them learn the inquiry process.

I Wonder Data Sheet

big science
for little hands

Name _____

I wonder _____

_____

What I Plan to Do

What I Found Out

Stop and Reflect

After investigating more about crayons, review with children what they have discovered so far. Keep a record of the children's ideas to show the progress of their learning.

Guide the reflection process by asking
- What can you tell people about crayons and wax?
- What new things did you discover in your work?
- Were you surprised by anything that happened during your test?
- What did you notice?
- What else about crayons and wax would you like to know and find out? How could you do that?

What to look for
Children have now had a variety of experiences with crayons and wax. They have explored the materials with teacher guidance and then more independently. During reflection, listen for details about their experiences. Some children may focus on the processes they used to explore. Other children may focus on the results and their observations of the experiments themselves.

Encourage children to be descriptive and offer ideas to explain what they have learned.

Part 5:
Application

What is the application phase?

In the application phase, learners apply and use their understandings in new settings and situations. The activities in this phase can also serve as assessment tools.

During application, children

- use their learning in different ways,

- represent learning in various ways,

- apply learning to new situations, and

- formulate new hypotheses and repeat the learning cycle.

The teacher's role is to

- create links for application in the world outside the classroom,

- help children apply learning to new situations, and

- provide meaningful situations in which children use what they have learned.

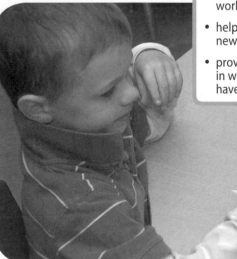

Application 1:
Let's Compare

Children apply what they've learned about crayons while comparing crayons to candles.

Duration

1 large group session

Purpose

- observe the properties of crayons and candles
- compare and contrast crayons and candles

What You Need

- poster board or large piece of paper
- candles in assorted shapes, sizes, and colors
- crayons
- paper
- magnifying lenses
- (optional) tape
- (optional) materials to determine whether a candle will melt or is waterproof (such as watercolor paints, hair dryer, and other items from previous activities)

Getting Ready

Create a class chart as shown below. For nonreaders, either draw pictures of candles and crayons or tape actual crayons and candles on the chart.

Be Safe

Remind children to keep candles and crayons out of their mouth.

Spotlight Vocabulary

- same/different
- compare

Example of class chart

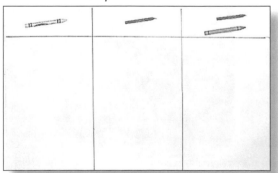

Begin

1. Show the class a collection of candles and ask them if these objects are crayons. Discuss with the children why these objects may or may not be crayons. Make a list of their comparisons on the class chart. (Don't worry if children are having trouble coming up with ideas. The class will revisit the list in step 4.)

   ### Questions to guide interest and enthusiasm:
   > *Are these crayons? Why or why not?*
   > *What tests can we do to find out if these are crayons?*

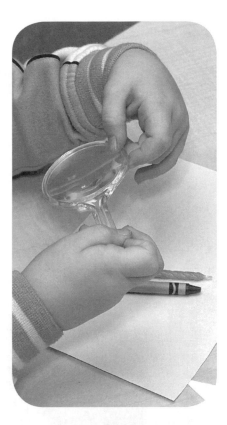

Continue

2. Give each child a candle, a crayon, and a magnifying lens. Have them take a closer look with a magnifying lens. What do they observe? Encourage them to use their senses.

   ### Questions to guide interest and enthusiasm:
   > *How are the candle and the crayon the same?*
   > *How are the candle and the crayon different?*

   ### Seen and heard:
   > *Children said, "Candles have fire," "They have a stem [wick]," and "They all have wax."*

3. Give each child a piece of paper to test the crayon and the candle. Let the children observe and discuss what happens when they try to write with each object. Children can also test the waterproof and melting abilities of the candle.

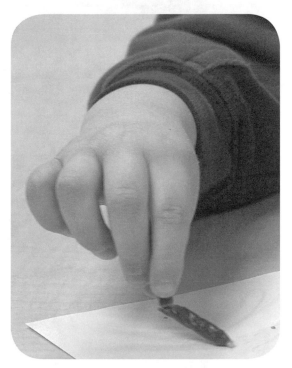

   ### Questions to guide interest and enthusiasm:
   > *What happens to the candle when you color?*
   > *What happens to the crayon when you color?*
   > *What happens to the paper when you color with the crayon and candle?*
   > *How is the candle like a crayon?*
   > *How is the candle not like a crayon?*

   ### Seen and heard:
   > *Children said, "Candles leave a mark" and "Crayons color better."*

Example answers for class chart

Candles	Crayons	Crayons and Candles
have strings (wicks)	have paper on them	wax
burns	Kids use them	lots of colors
give light	have names on them	made in factories
on birthday cakes		can melt
		waterproof
		can color with them

4. Ask the children how candles and crayons are the same. Ask the children what they discovered was different about candles and crayons. Encourage the children to use words they learned in their study of crayons. Add the children's observations to the class chart. Discuss and add ideas that the children may have missed. (See example.)

What to Look For

Children can explain what they have learned about crayons by comparing crayons to candles. Encourage the children to use descriptive words and details that reflect what they learned in previous activities. Listen for them to include Spotlight Vocabulary words in their discussion. Look for examples children may highlight as they explain their ideas.

Application 2:
Is This a Crayon?

Children apply what they've learned about crayons when comparing the properties of a mystery object and a crayon.

Duration

2 small group sessions and 1 large group session

Purpose

- compare properties of a mystery object and a commercial crayon
- use observations to decide if the mystery object is a crayon

What You Need

- materials for Getting Ready (including aluminum foil, pieces of crayon, metal tray, and oven) or uniquely shaped crayons such as Crayon Rocks™
- I Wonder Data Sheet for each child (See **Advanced Inquiry 2: I Wonder...** for a sample data sheet.)
- materials to test the mystery objects (such as squares of different materials, paper towels, watercolor paints, hair dryer, and other items from previous activities)
- assortment of crayons used in previous activities

Be Safe

Remind children not to put the mystery objects in their mouth.

Getting Ready

Make one mystery object for each small group of children as follows. (As an alternative, purchase unique-shaped crayons.)

1. Decide on a unique shape (such as a triangle, square, or rectangle) that is different from the shape of a crayon. Don't choose a circle because children saw melted crayon circles in **Inquiry 6: Major Meltdown**.

2. Make molds by forming a double thickness of aluminum foil into the unique shape. (For example, you can use a small box to form the shape as shown at right.) Be sure all molds are the same size and shape.

3. Put broken crayons of assorted colors into each mold and place the molds on a foil-lined metal tray.

4. Melt the crayons in an oven at 350° for 2–3 minutes.

5. Carefully remove molds from oven. Let cool to solidify. Peel off the foil.

Spotlight Vocabulary

- mystery
- same/different

Begin

1. Working in small groups, challenge the class by presenting a mystery object and asking, "Is this a crayon?" Let the children observe the mystery object and compare it to what they previously learned about crayons.

   Questions to guide interest and enthusiasm:
   > *Have you ever seen this object before?*
   > *What do you notice about it?*
   > *How is this object the same as a crayon? How is it different?*

2. Show children the class charts and materials from previous activities. Review what was done and discovered. Ask children to decide what experiments can be done to find out if the mystery object is a crayon. (See examples at left.) Help them use I Wonder Data Sheets from **Advanced Inquiry 2: I Wonder...** to record what they want to do for their investigations.

Examples

- Explore the way the mystery object colors on different materials (as in **Inquiries 2 and 3**).
- Color a circle with the mystery object and drop water on the circle to check water resistance (as in **Inquiry 5**).
- Try melting a piece of the mystery object with a hair dryer (as in **Inquiry 6**).
- Scrape off pieces of the mystery object onto wax paper and try to melt the pieces with a hair dryer (as in **Inquiry 6**).
- Duplicate the "I Wonder" investigations tried in **Advanced Inquiry 2**.

Continue

3. Let the children do the experiments they have planned with the mystery objects and compare results to their work with crayons. Have the children summarize their findings on the I Wonder Data Sheets.

4. Have each small group show their I Wonder Data Sheets to the class and share their findings. You may want to summarize results on a class chart as shown. After every group has presented, ask the class if the mystery object is a crayon.

Questions to guide the discussion:

> *What did you do with the mystery object and crayon?*

> *What happened?*

Seen and heard:

Children said, "It melted with a hair dryer," "Water doesn't stick," and "It's a crayon."

Example of class chart

Is this a crayon?	Feels like wax?	Waterproof?	Melts?
	Yes	Yes	Yes
	Yes	Yes	Yes

What to Look For

Listen to the children as they seek to answer the questions about whether the mystery object is a crayon. Encourage the children to apply what they learned about crayons in designing investigations to compare the mystery objects to crayons. Listen for the children to include Spotlight Vocabulary words in their discussion. Encourage the children to use details and actual observations to explain their answers.

Have More Fun

❏ Children can repeat this activity by comparing crayons to sidewalk chalk, nontoxic charcoal sticks (sold in art supply stores), or other mystery objects.

Testing sidewalk chalk

Stop and Reflect

What you need

- small pieces of paper
- pencils and crayons
- poster board or large sheet of paper

Reflection activity

Give each child a small piece of paper. Ask the children to draw or write one thing that they have learned from all of their investigations.

Bring the children together to show their papers and share their discoveries with the class. You may want to sort the papers into categories as children share. For example, one category could be about crayons and the other could be about wax. List the categories on the top of a poster board or large sheet of paper. Children can help you decide in which category each paper belongs. Attach the children's papers to the class chart in the appropriate category. When all have shared, display this class chart in the room.

Part 6:
Crayons Across the Curriculum

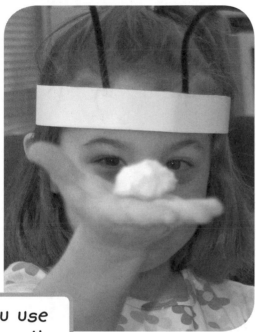

How can you use crayons across the curriculum?

This section includes fun ideas for extending children's learning with crayons into other learning in the classroom.

Across the Curriculum 1:
Writing to Learn

Children share their thoughts and knowledge about crayons and wax with their teacher, classmates, and families by creating pictures and stories that summarize what they learned through observation, exploration, and investigation.

Duration

1 small group session and 1 large group session

Purpose

- document ideas about crayons and wax
- create pictures to tell about crayons and wax
- write stories about crayons and wax

What You Need

- paper and illustration tools for children to create pictures
- class charts and examples of children's work from previous activities
- (optional) digital camera and printer or instant camera

Spotlight Vocabulary

Encourage children to use the Spotlight Vocabulary from previous activities.

Begin

1. Display previous class charts and examples of children's work. Meet with the children in small groups to improve participation and individual contributions. Ask children what they learned about crayons and wax. Tell children they will be making pages for a class book.

2. Have each child draw a picture showing something he or she learned about crayons. Write a brief caption under the picture based on the artist's own words.

3. You can also have children dictate stories based on what they learned. You may have several children contribute to a longer story or individual children tell their own stories. Encourage children to use the Spotlight Vocabulary from previous activities. If available, use a digital camera and printer or an instant camera to quickly add pictures of children and their work to the stories.

4. Assemble the pictures and stories into a class book. Remember to create a title and include children's names as authors.

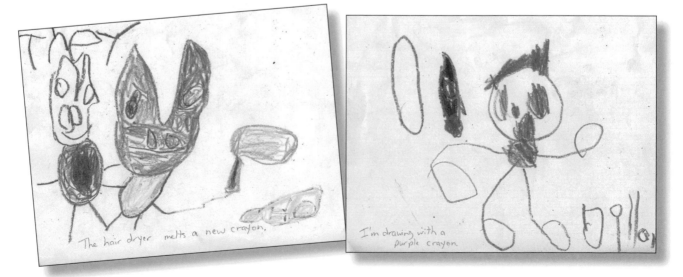

The hair dryer melts a new crayon.

I'm drawing with a purple crayon.

Continue

Helpful Hint

You can make copies of the class book for each child to take home. This empowers children to see the results of their work and to share their ideas just like scientists do. It also provides a valuable learning link between your classroom and children's homes.

5. Gather the children together and read the class book aloud. Highlight children's illustrations and contributions.

What to Look For

Watch for children to describe what they learned working with crayons and wax. Listen for them to include Spotlight Vocabulary words in their descriptions. Encourage the children to recall and articulate details from their experiences.

Across the Curriculum 2:
One Big Happy Family

Children hear a story and learn the importance of working together.

Duration
1 large group session

Purpose
- compare the class to a box of crayons
- realize that we are all good at different things
- realize that we can accomplish more by working together

What You Need
- *The Crayon Box that Talked,* by Shane DeRolf

Spotlight Vocabulary
- unique
- complete
- special
- wrapping

Begin

1. Emphasize to the class that people, like crayons, come in many different colors, sizes, and wrappings (clothes). However, it doesn't matter how we look. What's important is the kind of person each of us is.

2. Discuss the fact that everyone in the room not only looks different, but also is special in his or her own way. One by one, ask each member of the class to stand up. Call on different classmates to share something good about the person standing. Be sure the children talk about personality traits and not about appearances.

Seen and heard:

Children said, "He is always nice to me," "She is funny," "He is smart," and "She colors nice."

Continue

3. Read *The Crayon Box that Talked* to the class. Discuss the story with the children.

Questions to guide children's thinking and listening:

> *How did the crayons feel about each other at the beginning of the story?*

> *How did the crayons feel about each other at the end of the story?*

> *What was the green crayon good at coloring?*

> *What was the blue crayon good at coloring?*

> *What was the yellow crayon good at coloring?*

> *What was the white crayon good at coloring?*

4. Explain that each crayon was good at coloring one thing, but it took all of them together to make a complete picture. Compare the crayon box to the class again. Every child is good at certain things, but it takes everyone working together to make a happy classroom!

Have More Fun

❑ Suggest that each child become a talking crayon. What color do they want to be? What do they want to say?

❑ Ask each child to draw a design for their own crayon box. If you want to cover real crayon boxes with designs, cut strips of paper that can be colored by the children, then wrapped around crayon boxes and glued.

Across the Curriculum 3:
Book Adventures

Children learn what others think about crayons and wax by exploring children's literature.

Duration

several large group sessions

Purpose

- discover common ideas about crayons and wax in literature
- find out new information through literature

What You Need

- poster boards or large pieces of paper
- selection of both fiction and nonfiction children's literature on crayons
- (optional) copy machine, digital camera, instant camera, or computer with printer

Getting Ready

Prepare class charts for each of the books you are going to read. Ideally, attach images of the book covers to the charts. For example:

- Make a copy of the cover using a copy machine.
- Take a photograph of the cover using a digital or instant camera.
- Print a copy of the cover from an Internet site.

Spotlight Vocabulary

- author
- information
- opinion
- experience

Helpful Hint

Here are just a few ideas:
- *Harold and the Purple Crayon,* by Crockett Johnson
- *Bad Day at Riverbend,* by Chris Van Allsburg
- *My Crayons Talk,* by Patricia Hubbard
- *From Wax to Crayons,* by Robin Nelson
- *How a Crayon Is Made,* by Oz Charles

Begin

1. Explain to the children that authors write about their experiences. Here are some books where authors share their ideas about crayons. By reading these books and looking at the pictures, the class can learn what the authors know about crayons.

2. Take several large group sessions to read books aloud and share the pictures. Discuss each book and record student responses on the class charts prepared in Getting Ready. Afterwards, put the books and the class charts on display.

Questions to guide children's thinking and listening:

> *What ideas did the author have that we also discovered?*

> *What new information did the author give us about crayons?*

> *Which is your favorite part of the book? Why?*

Continue

3. Review the class charts. Ask the children to review and compare the books that were shared. Children may want to create a short summary of ideas that they can take home and share with their families.

Questions to guide the discussion:

> *What have you learned from these books?*

> *What book taught you the most?*

> *What book was the most fun?*

Seen and heard:

Children said, "I liked Harold," "I want to color cowboys," and "I wish my crayons talked."

What to Look For

Look for children to demonstrate, through verbal descriptions and ideas, their awareness that literature can reinforce experiences and offer new ideas. Sharing literature experiences with their families emphasizes the importance of literature for extending student learning.

Across the Curriculum 4:
Group Graph

The class creates a graph showing their favorite crayon colors.

Duration

1 large group session

Purpose

- share favorite crayon colors (and why)
- compile a simple bar graph

What You Need

- poster board or large piece of paper
- 8 crayons (red, yellow, blue, green, pink, purple, brown, and orange)
- (optional) graphs for each child to fill out (See master at the end of this activity.)

Getting Ready

- Prepare two large class graphs. Title one graph "Our Favorite Crayon Colors" as shown at bottom right. This graph will be used in step 2. Title the other graph "Practice Graph." Use crayons in appropriate colors to fill in data from a make-believe class. This graph will be used in step 4.
- If children will be filling out their own graphs, make extra copies in case some children need to start over. (Use the master at the end of this activity.)

Spotlight Vocabulary

- favorite
- most
- graph
- second
- fewest
- data
- color words (such as red, yellow, blue, green)

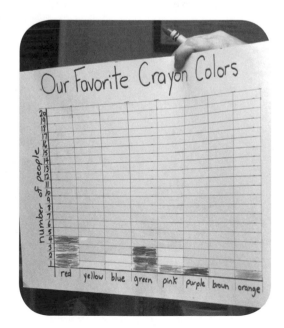

Begin

1. Explain to the class that you want to make a graph showing everyone's favorite crayon color. First the class has to collect data. Show the children the eight crayon colors. Tell the children that they will be asked to stand up, pick a favorite crayon color, and tell why.

2. As each child shares his or her favorite color, color the appropriate box on the graph using the appropriate crayon. If you'd like, children can follow along by coloring in their own graphs. Since this may be the children's first experience with graphing, make sure they understand to start with the bottom square and move upward as more children pick the color.

Seen and heard:

Children said, "Pink because it's always bright," "Green because grass is green," and "I like red because I like juice."

Continue

3. After completing the graph, ask questions to analyze the data.

    Questions to guide children's thinking and listening:
    > *What color did the most children like?*
    > *How do you know?*
    > *What color came in second?*
    > *What color had the fewest votes?*

4. Give the children more practice by showing them the make-believe graph. Ask questions to analyze the data.

    Questions to guide the analysis:
    > *What is the favorite color in this class?*
    > *What is the least favorite color?*
    > *How do you know?*

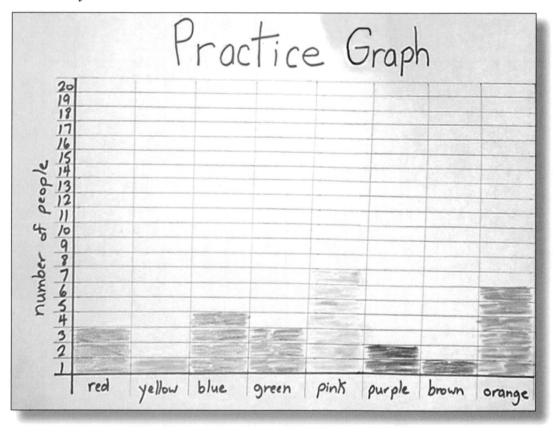

name _____

OUR FAVORITE CRAYON COLORS

	red	yellow	blue	green	pink	purple	brown	orange

number of students

Across the Curriculum 5:
What Are the Chances?

Children make predictions about crayons and build foundation concepts and skills for an understanding of probability.

Duration
1 large group session

Purpose
- predict and understand the likelihood that certain color crayons will be pulled from a bag

What You Need
- poster board or large piece of paper
- index cards
- bag
- Choose a bag that you can't see through, such as a brown lunch bag.
- at least 6 crayons (3 red, 1 yellow, 1 blue, and 1 green)

Getting Ready
- Prepare a class chart as shown at right. Cut slits to hold an index card.
- Prepare an index card as shown below for each crayon group that will go in the bag. (See steps 2, 4, 5, and 6.)

Spotlight Vocabulary
- more likely
- predict
- probably
- color words (such as red, yellow, blue, green)

Example of class chart

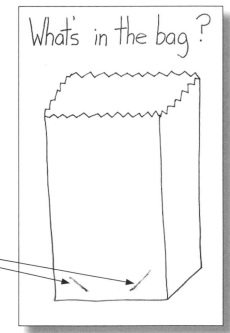

What's in the bag?

Cut slits.

Example of index cards

Begin

1. Show the children a bag that they can't see through and explain to them that they will try to predict the color of crayons pulled out of the bag.

   ### Seen and heard:
   A child said, "Wow! We must be magic!"

2. On the class chart, hang an index card showing three red crayons. Show the children that the bag is empty, then put three red crayons in the bag. Ask the children specific questions about what you might pull out of the bag.

   ### Questions to guide the inquiry:
   > *Do you think I will pull out a green crayon? Why?*
   > *Do you think I will pull out a blue crayon? Why?*
   > *Do you think I will pull out a red crayon? Why?*

3. Pull the crayons out of the bag one at a time to show that you always get red.

Continue

4. Place the three red crayons back in the bag and add one yellow crayon. Hang an index card showing three red crayons and one yellow crayon on the class chart so the children can remember what crayons are in the bag now. Before and while pulling the crayons out of the bag one at a time, ask the children specific questions about what you might pull out of the bag. Lead the children to conclude that there are more red crayons than yellow crayons, so you are more likely to pull out a red crayon.

Questions to guide the inquiry:

> *Do you think I will pull out a green crayon? Why?*

> *Do you think I will pull out a yellow crayon? Why?*

> *What color will I probably pull out? Why?*

Helpful Hint

Although some children will not understand that you are more likely to pull a red crayon out than a yellow one in step 4, most children will become very enthusiastic about predicting which color will be pulled out next.

5. Remove all the crayons from the bag and put in one yellow, one blue, one red, and one green. Change the class chart by removing and adding the appropriate index cards. Before and while pulling the crayons out of the bag one at a time, ask the children specific questions about what you might pull out of the bag.

Questions to guide the inquiry:

> *Do you think I will pull out a black crayon? Why?*

> *Do you think I will pull out a yellow crayon? Why?*

> *Do you think I will pull out a blue crayon? Why?*

> *Do you think I'll pull out a brown crayon? Why?*

> *Do you think I am more likely to pull out a red crayon than a green one? Why?*

Seen and heard:

> *Children said, "Pick me. I'm red," "No, pick me. I'm green," and "Yeah, you picked me."*

6. Repeat with other crayon combinations and similar questions.

Across the Curriculum 6:
Buzzing About Bees

Children discover things about bees and natural beeswax.

Duration

several large group sessions

Purpose

- explore bees and beeswax
- find out new information through various sources

What You Need

- *Busy, Buzzy Bees,* by Allan Fowler, or similar resource
- real honeycomb
- ☞ *Chunks of honeycomb (sometimes called comb honey) are available at health food stores.*
- materials to build beehives (such as tables and sheets)
- cotton balls
- at least 30 clear plastic cups
- (optional) antennae made from pipe cleaners and heavy paper (See photo at top left.)

Spotlight Vocabulary

- bee
- nectar
- honeycomb
- beeswax

Helpful Hint

You can serve honeycomb-shaped cereal for a snack today.

Begin

1. Point out that beeswax is used to make certain kinds of crayons. Read *Busy, Buzzy Bees* or a similar resource to the class.

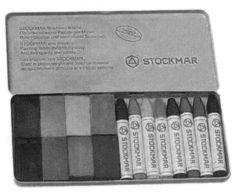

2. Show the children a real honeycomb. Point out that bees make honeycombs from beeswax. If possible, you can also arrange a visit from a beekeeper or other expert who can tell the children all about bees and beeswax. (Contact an area university or cooperative extension service to locate such an expert.)

Continue

3. Make "beehives" by draping tables with sheets to enclose the area under the table. Create a doorway for each beehive by folding up one edge of the sheet. Place piles of cotton balls (representing nectar found in flowers) around the room for children to collect in step 4. Divide the children into groups and assign each group one beehive.

4. Tell children to pretend to be buzzing bees that are gathering nectar to make food (honey). First, guide children to make honeycombs in their beehives by lining up plastic cups in even rows like the hexagonal wax cells in honeycomb. (See photo below.) Now the children can buzz around the room, gather nectar cotton balls, return to their beehives, and place the nectar in the honeycomb cups. Be sure each child visits many cotton ball piles and only takes one cotton ball from each pile to better represent how bees travel from flower to flower. Tell the children they can save the honey to "eat" during the long winter months when there are no flowers.

What to Look For

Look for children to apply what they learned from the book about bees during their creative dramatics. Encourage children to provide details using the Spotlight Vocabulary words.

Across the Curriculum 7:
Sandpaper Printing

Now that the children have learned about different properties of crayons, the experience of heat printing with crayons will take on new dimensions.

Duration

several small group sessions and 1 large group session

Purpose

- learn techniques for fabric printing using an iron and crayons
- create pieces of art

What You Need

- sample of sandpaper printing prepared in Getting Ready
- assortment of crayons
- light-colored sandpaper
- light-colored muslin or cotton fabric
- iron and ironing board for teacher use only
- brown paper (such as lunch bags)
- permanent marker to write student names on fabric
- (optional) samples of different types of art printing
- (optional) music

Be Safe

Keep the ironing area away from high traffic areas. Be careful with the electrical cord. Remind children to stay away from hot appliances.

Getting Ready

Test the procedures you will do with the class to become familiar with the steps and to make art samples for the class to look at in step 1.

Spotlight Vocabulary

- sandpaper
- print
- fabric
- iron
- design

Begin

1. Explain to the children that they will be putting designs on fabric in a special way. Show children the art samples you prepared in Getting Ready. Explain that first the class will color on sandpaper and then you will iron the sandpaper to transfer the wax designs onto fabric.

Continue

2. Ask children to color a design on sandpaper. Encourage them to heavily color and fill in areas with color for best results. You can play music while the children color to stimulate creativity.

3. Away from the children, place brown paper on an ironing board. On top of the brown paper, add a sandpaper drawing with the wax design facing up. Cover the design with a piece of fabric and top with another layer of brown paper. Iron the "sandwich" with medium heat for about 10–30 seconds. (You can peek to make sure the wax has transferred to the fabric, but put the fabric back over the sandpaper so the children will be surprised in step 4.) Repeat for all sandpaper drawings.

4. After all the sandpaper/fabric sandwiches cool, gather the class together. Let the children lift the fabric off the sandpaper to reveal their designs. Ask the children to explain what happened. Have the children share their work with the class.

Questions to guide the discussion:

> *What happens to crayon wax when you rub the crayon on sandpaper?*
> *What happens to crayon wax when it gets hot?*
> *How did the crayon wax get from the sandpaper to the fabric?*

Seen and heard:

Children said, "It gets wax on it," "It melts," and "My picture moved to the white."

What to Look For

Look for children to incorporate lines and color to make creative art pieces. Listen for detailed, descriptive words as children explain how they used crayons, sandpaper, and fabric to produce their artwork. Make sure children realize that heat from the iron melted the wax so their designs went from the sandpaper to the fabric.

Part 7: Science for Young Learners

How should we teach science to young children?

This section contains information on developmentally appropriate science instruction for young children, including fundamental concepts and process skills, inquiry-based science, teaching with learning cycles, and documenting children's learning.

Why Early Childhood Science?

Why bother with science in early childhood? Young children can't memorize the geologic periods or understand chemical reactions. Learning ABCs and how to share, listen, and even tie shoes, is a challenging business! Plus, the school day is too short to accomplish all we have to do now. Why not wait until children are older to introduce science?

The National Science Education Standards emphasize that all children can learn science and that all children should have the opportunity to become scientifically literate. In *Science in Early Childhood: Developing and Acquiring Fundamental Concepts and Skills,* Karen Lind writes "In order for this learning to happen, the effort to introduce children to the essential experiences of science inquiry and explorations must begin at an early age." (Lind, 1999)

Reaching Potentials: Transforming Early Childhood Curriculum and Assessment (from the National Association for the Education of Young Children) summarizes what developmentally-appropriate science instruction for young children is…and is not. The authors use the term "sciencing" to convey the child's active involvement in learning about science and to emphasize process in effective science teaching.

For Children 3 through 8, Developmentally Appropriate Sciencing...	
Is	**Is Not**
actively participating	memorizing a lot of facts
handling materials	watching the teacher do most of the demonstrating and handling of objects
controlling their own actions	
investigating familiar phenomena	studying content with no link to their knowledge or experience
reflecting on teachers' open-ended questions	being restricted by closed, single-right-answer questioning or being told what to expect
observing the results of their own actions	lacking opportunities to observe the results of their own actions
experiencing both planned and spontaneous opportunities	experiencing science only as teacher-planned activities
investigating and working individually or in small groups	participating in science activities only in a large group
investigating the range of basic concepts	learning about only one or two concepts
exploring a variety of content from life, earth, and physical sciences	learning only limited content
having their knowledge and skill assessed in multiple ways	having their knowledge and skills assessed only by written tests

Reaching Potentials: Transforming Early Childhood Curriculum and Assessment, Vol 2. "Transforming Science Curriculum," 1995, S. Kilmer and H. Hofman, pg. 62. Reproduced with permission of the National Association for the Education of Young Children.

When presented in a way that is meaningful for young minds, early childhood science education provides the foundation for a lifetime of science learning both in and out of school. The goal of the *Big Science for Little Hands* series is to help young children develop an understanding of fundamental concepts about the physical world and the fundamental process skills suitable for their developmental level.

Fundamental Concepts

The fundamental concepts allow children to organize their experiences with the physical world into meaningful patterns—the beginning of true science learning. How do children develop an awareness of these fundamental concepts? They need repeated, personal experiences with materials and events from their everyday world and the tools—in the form of process skills—to help them make sense of these experiences and the world around them.

The activities in this book provide a specific progression of experiences that help children build an understanding of the fundamental concepts listed below. This progression is in the form of a learning cycle. (See page 120 for a discussion of learning cycles.)

(See page 120 for a discussion of learning cycles.)

Fundamental Concepts	
Fundamental Concepts about the Physical World for the Early Childhood Level	**Examples of Use in Activities**
Objects and events have observable characteristics.	In **Exploration 1: A Closer Look at Crayons,** children learn that objects have observable characteristics as they explore crayons with their senses of touch, smell, hearing, and sight.
A person can act on objects or materials to change them and observe the results of their action.	In **Inquiry 6: Major Meltdown,** children find that their teacher's action, heating the crayons with a hair dryer, can change the crayons by making them warm and liquid. Once cool, the crayons change again and become solid, but have a different shape than at the start.
The physical world has patterns that help a person predict what will happen next.	By the time they reach **Application 2: Is This a Crayon?,** children have observed patterns of events that help them decide how to test whether the mystery object is a crayon and how to interpret the results of their tests.

Fundamental Process Skills

Each activity in this book helps children develop one or more of the process skills appropriate for the early childhood level. How we define these process skills is important, because what one person understands to be "measuring" or "organizing" may not be developmentally

Process Skill Power

"Although young children are not methodical, they naturally use one or more [process skills] as they investigate everything that attracts their attention. The early childhood teacher's job is to increase awareness and use of these skills."

Sally Kilmer and Helenmarie Hofman, 1995

appropriate for this level. Review the following list and definitions carefully. Note that young children can begin practicing simpler versions of intermediate-level process skills.

Process Skills	
Fundamental Process Skills for the Early Childhood Level	
Observing	Using the senses to gather information about objects or events is the most fundamental of the scientific thinking processes. Rich observation experiences enable children to create a repertoire of possible properties that make up objects or events and form a foundation for comparing and organizing.
Communicating	Sharing oral or written ideas and descriptions in a way that helps others understand the meaning.
Comparing	Examining the character of objects in order to discover similarities or differences. Comparing builds upon the process of observing and begins in younger children with comparing two objects at a time.
Measuring	Comparing objects to arbitrary units that may or may not be standardized. Measuring skills begin to develop as children compare objects to one another (such as bigger/smaller, hotter/colder). The skill then extends to comparing objects to nonstandard units of measure (such as one block equals three counting bears). Beginning in primary grades, children can understand the value of using standard units such as pounds and inches.
Organizing	This skill includes grouping, classifying, seriating (ordering objects along a continuum), and sequencing (placing events one after another so that they tell a logical story). • Grouping begins at about age 3 with resemblance sorting: putting objects together (in pairs, piles, or chains) on the basis of one-to-one correspondence. Each pair or pile may be based on a different kind of resemblance, such as red objects in one pile and square ones in another. • Consistent and exhaustive sorting starts at about age 6, when a child will use up all the pieces in a set using one consistent rule for grouping, such as color. • Multiple membership classifying—the ability to place an object into more than one category at the same time or into one category based on two or more simultaneous properties—begins at about age 8.
Simple Versions of Intermediate Process Skills for Early Childhood Children	
Reasonable guessing	More than a simple guess, based on prior knowledge. For example, perceiving a pattern emerging and surmising how it will continue. Reasonable guessing is a step towards predicting.
Early data collecting and interpreting	Can include counting and making pictures to represent information discovered by exploration. Children can reflect upon these results together. Teachers can model these process skills with the children as ways to organize information found in exploration and investigation. This skill gives purpose to activities and further experiments.

Facilitating "Sciencing"

Spontaneous sciencing occurs every day. Whenever children see something of interest, wonder about it, and investigate to answer their questions, sciencing is going on. These experiences are certainly valuable, but "what children gain can be enhanced and increased by planning. Both the classroom environment and our teaching strategies should encourage active sciencing." (Kilmer, 1995)

Teachers are the role models and facilitators of sciencing. As models, teachers need to display all of the behaviors identified as outcomes for the children. "Teachers are not expected to know all there is to know about sciencing. What is important is that the teacher be open, enthusiastic, and willing to wonder 'What happens if…?'" (Kilmer, 1995)

Science learning flourishes when teachers facilitate a classroom atmosphere that respects each child's contribution, supports inquiry and experimentation without passing judgements about right and wrong, and embraces "mistakes" as opportunities for new discoveries. Strategic comments and questions can focus and extend children's thinking. By carefully observing a child's behavior, teachers can help put into words an unspoken question a child may be thinking about.

One effective technique for helping children try new approaches to investigations is to join the child in their activity and begin by imitating what the child is doing. The adult then gradually adds something new to his or her actions. "If, for instance, the focus is on bubbles, after the child has had time to explore blowing bubbles in various ways but has not spontaneously used some of the different bubble-makers provided, the teacher sits beside the child. After using the same bubble-maker as the child is using, the teacher begins to try different ones." (Kilmer, 1995) Frequently, the child will notice the teacher's behavior and expand his or her own exploration.

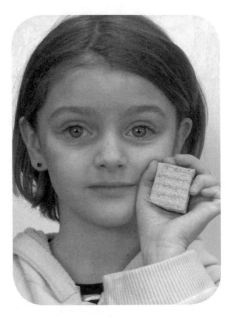

Self-Directed Inquiry

As children develop and practice the process skills and inquiry modeled by the teacher, their abilities to initiate, plan, and conduct self-directed inquiry grows. Children "begin the process of asking and answering their own questions, which is at the heart of the inquiry experience." (Villavicencio, 2000)

Joanna Villavicencio's experiences doing self-directed inquiry with 4- and 5-year-old children shows the ability of young children to benefit from these opportunities. As children explore, she guides them to follow a five-part structure that helps organize their investigations:

- form a question;
- make a plan;
- do the investigation;
- record and report; and
- reflect, revisit, and plan again.

Until they have experience with inquiry, children often have difficulty asking questions that can be tested. Teachers need to actively facilitate children's efforts to ask such questions. Wendy Cheong writes, "While watching the children explore, I encourage them to ask questions about whatever seems curious to them…I support them in various ways. For example, I model techniques and ask a lot of open-ended questions, such as: "Can you tell me what you are trying to find out with this instrument?" Eventually, the children get used to hearing the kinds of questions that can lead to investigations." (Cheong, 2000)

Jane Bresnik models this process by asking questions that begin with "I wonder," such as "I wonder what will happen if I hold the ramp higher?" The words "I wonder…" become the first part of a template Jane uses to help children organize their investigations. Children state their "I wonder" question, explain their plan, conduct their tests, and then explain what happened using the "I found out…" prompt. (Bresnik, 2000)

As children begin their investigations, teachers need to work with them by observing, questioning, supporting their efforts, and redirecting their investigations. Reporting the results of investigations to others is an important step. Joanna Villavicencio explains that "In the beginning, the children have a hard time articulating their discoveries, so I help them find the right words to explain what they discovered…I have seen how language develops during the inquiry process. As children share what they see, they find words to express and refine their thinking." (Villavicencio, 2000)

How Children Learn

Current research on how humans learn is helping educators understand what fosters learning and how to improve ineffective or even detrimental aspects of teaching. In "How New Science Curriculums Reflect Brain Research," Lawrence Lowery describes a view of learning based on research in the cognitive sciences:

- learners construct understanding for themselves,
- to understand is to know relationships, and
- knowing relationships depends on having prior knowledge.

The brain needs data it can use to construct knowledge. Our senses are like windows that allow the brain to collect and store data with everything we do, perceive, think, or feel. "Learners do not simply mirror what they are told or what they read. The brain does not store a picture of an event. It does not directly record anything that is shown." (Lowery, 1998) What the brain does do is store information clustered into different areas of the brain with networks of pathways connecting these places. For example, sensory perceptions are grouped in different places in the brain—shapes, colors, movements, textures, and aromas are each stored in their own places. Components of language are also stored in their own places—nouns in one place, verbs in another.

"As the brain constructs connections among brain cells, it connects the organization of words, objects, events, and relationships…The result is that human knowledge is stored in clusters and organized within the brain into systems that people use to interpret familiar situations and reason about new ones." (Lowery, 1998) The more avenues that children have to receive data through the senses, the more connections their brain will make.

Knowledge is constructed through experience, but the quality of that construction is greatly affected by how well the brain organizes and stores relationships. For example, a child exploring a magnet experiences the following relationships:

- a relationship between the learner and the object (how the hand and arm are positioned to hold the magnet);
- cause and effect relationships between the learner's actions and observed results (how the magnet can be moved and manipulated); and
- cause and effect relationships in an interaction between objects in the environment (how other objects behave in the presence of the magnet).

As exploration continues, "learners try to link new perceptions to what they have already constructed in the brain's storage systems. They use this prior knowledge to interpret the new material in terms of established knowledge." (Lowery, 1998) Bits of information that are not integrated with prior knowledge are forgotten. The more opportunities children have to explore relationships among objects and ideas and to use their prior knowledge, the richer and more permanent their constructions of knowledge will be. This is accomplished through rehearsals—reinforcing what has been learned while adding something new.

The activities in this book have been thoughtfully constructed to address what we know about how children learn and to provide the types of experiences described in this section. Doing these activities with young children will help to build a foundation for a lifetime of science learning and exploration.

Find Out More

Bredekamp, Sue, and Teresa Rosegrant, Eds. *Reaching Potentials: Appropriate Curriculum and Assessment for Young Children.* Vol. 1. Washington, DC: National Association for the Education of Young Children (NAEYC), 1992.

Bredekamp, Sue, and Teresa Rosegrant, Eds. *Reaching Potentials: Transforming Early Childhood Curriculum and Assessment.* Vol. 2. Washington, DC: National Association for the Education of Young Children (NAEYC), 1995.

Connect: Inquiry Learning Issue Vol. 13(4), 2000: pgs. 1–26.

Dialogue on Early Childhood Science, Mathematics, and Technology Education; American Association for the Advancement of Science (AAAS) Project 2061: Washington, DC, 1999.

Lind, Karen. *Exploring Science in Early Childhood: A Developmental Approach.* Albany, NY: Delmar Publishers, 2000.

Lowery, Lawrence. "**How New Science Curriculums Reflect Brain Research.**" *Educational Leadership* Vol. 56(3), 1998: pgs. 26–30.

Lowery, Lawrence. *The Scientific Thinking Process.* Berkeley, CA: Lawrence Hall of Science, 1992.

National Association for the Education of Young Children (NAEYC). *Developmentally Appropriate Practice in Early Childhood Programs Serving Children from Birth through Age 8.* 1997. Available: www.naeyc.org/about/positions/daptoc.asp (accessed January 31, 2008).

National Research Council. *National Science Education Standards: Observe, Interact, Change, Learn.* Washington, DC: National Academy Press, 1996.

Good Science at Any Age

The list below was developed by teachers and administrators participating in the Vermont Elementary Science Project. They write, "The intent is not to use this guide as a checklist, but as a statement of what we value in the areas of science processes, science dispositions, and science concept development. We urge you to capture evidence of your own students engaging in these indicators."

Inquiry-Based Science: What Does It Look Like?

When students are doing inquiry based science, an observer will see that

Children view themselves as scientists in the process of learning.

- Children look forward to doing science.
- They demonstrate a desire to learn more.
- They seek to collaborate and work cooperatively with their peers.
- They are confident in doing science; they demonstrate a willingness to modify ideas, take risks, and display healthy skepticism.

Children accept an "invitation to learn" and readily engage in the exploration process.

- Children exhibit curiosity and ponder observations.
- They move around, selecting and using the materials they need.
- They take the opportunity and the time to try out their own ideas.

Children plan and carry out investigations.

- Children design a way to try out their ideas, not expecting to be told what to do.
- They plan ways to verify, extend, or discard ideas.
- They carry out investigations by handling materials, observing, measuring, and recording data.

Children communicate using a variety of methods.

- Children express ideas in a variety of ways, such as with journals, reporting, drawing, graphing, and charting.
- They listen, speak, and write about science with parents, teachers, and peers.
- They use the language of the processes of science.
- They communicate their level of understanding of concepts that they have developed to date.

Children propose explanations and solutions and build a store of concepts.

- Children offer explanations from a store of previous knowledge.
- They use investigations to answer their own questions.
- They sort information and decide what information is important.
- They are willing to revise explanations as they gain new knowledge.

Children raise questions.

- Children ask questions (verbally or through actions).
- They use questions to lead them to investigations that generate further questions or ideas.
- They value and enjoy asking questions as an important part of science.

Children use observation.

- Children observe, as opposed to just looking.
- They see details; they detect sequences and events; they notice changes, similarities, and differences.
- They make connections to previously held ideas.

Children critique their science practices.

- They use indicators to assess their own work.
- They report their strengths and weaknesses.
- They reflect with their peers.

The Vermont Elementary Science Project (VESP) is located at Trinity College, McAuley Hall, Burlington, VT 05401; (802) 658-3664. VESP is a grant awarded to The NETWORK, Inc., Andover, MA, by the National Science Foundation.

Teaching with Learning Cycles

What are learning cycles and why teach with them? A learning cycle is a structured approach to science teaching that takes into account what we know about how children learn. The work of researchers such as Piaget, Vygotsky, and Lowery has taught us that children acquire new concepts and skills by building upon what they already know and are able to do. This process is called the construction of knowledge.

In *Guidelines for Appropriate Curriculum Content and Assessment in Programs Serving Children Ages 3 through 8,* the National Association for the Education of Young Children (NAEYC) recommends that "the curriculum provides conceptual frameworks for children so that their mental constructions based on prior knowledge become more complex over time." (NAEYC, 1990)

Often, the early childhood science curriculum consists of conceptually unrelated activities chosen to coordinate with the seasons of the year or some other theme. NAEYC encourages science curriculum that builds conceptually upon itself rather than only coordinating with such a theme: "As in menu planning, the individual recipes may be appropriate and valuable, but without a framework and organization, they may fail to provide the opportunity for rich conceptual development that is likely with a more coherent, thoughtful approach."

Providing this "coherent, thoughtful approach" can be a challenge, but the structure of a learning cycle gives teachers a framework for doing so. In *How New Science Curriculums Reflect Brain Research,* Lawrence Lowery explains, "The learning cycle is viewed as a way to take students on a quest for knowledge that leads to the construction of knowledge. It is used both as a curriculum development procedure and a teaching strategy." A learning cycle creates a sequence of instructions that provides "a rehearsal of prior knowledge constructions, thus making them more permanent, and provides something new that the brain can assimilate into its prior construction, thus enriching and extending those constructions."

Typically, a learning cycle has four phases, each with one or more activities. The phases of the learning cycle are summarized on the following pages. This summary is adapted from NAEYC's *Guidelines for Appropriate Curriculum Content and Assessment in Programs Serving Children Ages 3 through 8.*

Process Skill Power

"The sequence of... instruction is important to move children from being novices to becoming experts. Each new challenge does two things: provides a rehearsal of prior knowledge constructions, thus making them more permanent, and provides something new that the brain can assimilate into its prior construction, thus enriching and extending those constructions."

Lawrence Lowery, 1998

Phase 1: Awareness—What's in my world? What do I know?

The awareness phase helps children develop broad recognition of the parameters of the learning—events, objects, people, or concepts.

During awareness, children
- experience,
- awaken curiosity, and
- develop an interest.

The teacher's role is to
- create a rich environment;
- provide opportunities by introducing new objects, people, events, or concepts;
- invite and encourage interest by posing a problem or question;
- respond to children's interest; and
- show interest and enthusiasm.

Phase 2: Exploration—What more can I find out about my world?

The exploration phase enables children to construct personal meaning through sensory experiences with objects, people, events, or concepts.

During exploration, children
- observe and explore materials,
- collect information, and
- construct their own understandings and meanings from their experiences.

The teacher's role is to
- facilitate, support, and enhance exploration;
- ask open-ended questions;
- respect children's thinking and rule systems;
- allow for constructive error; and
- model ways to organize information from experiences.

Phase 3: Inquiry—How can I research new things?

The inquiry phase of the learning cycle enables children to deepen and refine their understanding.

During inquiry, children
- examine,
- investigate,
- propose explanations,
- compare own thinking with that of others,
- generalize, and
- relate to prior learning.

The teacher's role is to
- help children refine understanding,
- ask more focused questions,
- provide information when requested, and
- help children make connections among prior experiences and their investigations.

Phase 4: Application—How can I apply what I learn?

In the application phase, learners apply and use their understandings in new settings and situations. The activities in this phase can also serve as assessment tools.

During application, children
- use their learning in different ways,
- represent learning in various ways,
- apply learning to new situations, and
- formulate new hypotheses and repeat learning cycle.

The teacher's role is to
- create links for application in the world outside the classroom,
- help children apply learning to new situations, and
- provide meaningful situations in which children use what they have learned.

Throughout the learning cycle, open-ended questions encourage the child to put into words what he or she is observing, doing, and wondering. When teaching with a learning cycle, teachers can ask focusing questions to support each phase of the learning cycle.

Find Out More

Barman, Charles R. "**Teaching Teachers: The Learning Cycle.**" *Science and Children* Vol. 26(7), 1989: pgs. 30–32.

Beisenherz, Paul C. "**Explore, Invent, and Apply.**" *Science and Children* Vol. 28(4), 1991: pgs. 30–32.

Marek, Edmund A., and Ann M. L. Cavallo. ***The Learning Cycle: Elementary School Science and Beyond.*** Portsmouth, NH: Heinemann, 1997.

National Association of Early Childhood Specialists in State Departments of Education (NAECS/SDE). ***Guidelines for Appropriate Curriculum Content and Assessment in Programs Serving Children Ages 3 through 8***. Produced jointly with NAECS/SDE and the NAEYC and adopted by both Associations in 1990. Published in ***Young Children***, March 1991, pp. 21–38 and in ***Reaching Potentials: Appropriate Curriculum and Assessment for Young Children,*** Volume 1, 1991, pp. 9–27. Available: *naecs.crc.uiuc.edu/position/currcont.html* (accessed January 30, 2008).

Documenting Learning

The book *Windows on Learning: Documenting Young Children's Work* (Helm, Beneke, and Steinheimer, 1998) begins with this idea: "Documenting children's learning may be one of the most valuable skills a teacher can develop today." The preprimary schools of Reggio Emilia, Italy, have been attracting worldwide attention for more than a decade. In these schools, documentation of children's experience is a standard part of classroom practice. "Documentation practices in Reggio Emilia preprimary schools provide inspiring examples of the importance of displaying children's work with great care and attention to both the content and aesthetic aspects of the display." (Katz, 1996)

Through documentation, teachers help themselves and others see and understand the learning that is taking place. Documentation serves many purposes, providing

- evidence for monitoring each child's growth and development and reliably assessing progress;
- a method of meeting accountability requirements and communicating with parents and administrators;
- evidence to the child of the importance of his or her work to teachers and parents;
- a means of sharing results with children and capturing their interest;
- opportunities to enhance children's memory of their prior work; and
- a mechanism for teachers to evaluate and improve curriculum and teaching methods, thus becoming producers of research.

"Documenting Early Science Learning" (Jones and Courtney, 2002) recommends that documentation and assessment of children's work in science follow a five-stage cycle. Teachers begin by identifying science objectives: what children should experience, explore, and understand. Next, teachers collect evidence of children's learning according to three guiding principles:

- **Variety of forms of evidence.** Children vary in how they demonstrate their understanding. Types of evidence collected in early childhood classrooms usually include drawings, some with comments dictated to the teacher; photographs; and a record of children's language, particularly in response to open-ended questions.

- **Evidence over a period of time.** A single piece of evidence captures only one moment in time. However, children's understandings of big concepts are not established with a single experience. At a particular moment, a child may be struggling with an idea or question. When added to evidence collected over a period of weeks or months, that single piece of evidence becomes part of a larger picture of development.

- **The understanding of groups of children as well as individuals.** Capturing group conversations at the introduction of a topic can give teachers a sense of what prior experiences, understandings, and misconceptions the group as a whole shares. Science is a social activity, where the sharing of questions, methods, and results is an essential part of the process. Through this sharing, the class as a whole comes to new understandings about a concept. Recording group conversations at the end of a unit can document this outcome.

After collecting evidence of children's learning, the teacher looks closely at the material collected and describes the knowledge represented by the evidence. Doing this step without judgment (such as focusing on what is missing or incorrect) takes practice. Now the children's work can be compared to the standards and goals that the teacher previously identified. Finally, this new information and understanding help the teacher improve instruction and curriculum.

Some early childhood programs use established methods for documentation and assessment. One popular method is the Work Sampling System. It consists of three complementary components: developmental guidelines and checklists, portfolios of children's work, and summary reports by teachers. Assessment takes place three times a year and is meant to place children's work within a broad, developmental perspective. Training to use this system helps teachers develop skills in nonjudgmental recording of behavior. The structure of the system helps teachers organize the collection and evaluation of children's work.

Find Out More

Gandini, Lella. "**Fundamentals of the Reggio Emilia Approach to Early Childhood Education.**" *Young Children* Vol. 49(1), 1993: pgs. 4–8.

Helm, Judy, Sallee Beneke, and Kathy Steinheimer. *Windows on Learning: Documenting Young Children's Work.* New York: Teachers College Press, 1998.

Hoisington, Cynthia. "**Using Photographs to Support Children's Science Inquiry.**" *Young Children* Vol. 57(5), 2002: pgs. 26–32.

Jones, Jacqueline, and Rosalea Courtney. "**Documenting Early Science Learning.**" *Young Children* Vol. 57(5), 2002: pgs. 34–40.

Katz, Lilian G. "**Impressions of Reggio Emilia Preschools.**" *Young Children* Vol. 45(6), 1990: pgs. 10–11.

Meisels, S.J., et al. *An Overview: The Work Sampling System.* Ann Arbor, MI: Rebus Planning Associates, 1994.

Part 8: All About Crayons and Wax

What are some interesting facts about crayons and wax?

This section includes some interesting background information about the history of crayons, manufacture of crayons, and facts about wax. You may choose to share some of this information with the children when appropriate during the class sessions.

Crayons Are Made from Wax

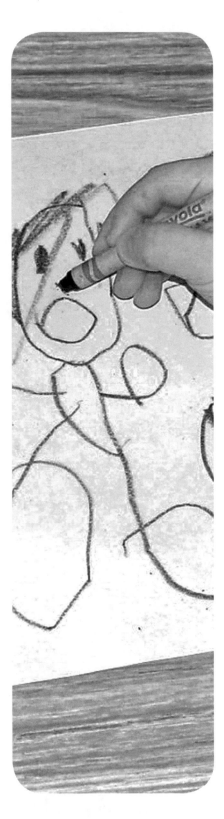

Most children begin drawing at an early age, and crayons are usually the first drawing instrument they learn to use. Using crayons helps children develop the skills to hold a pencil correctly. Crayons are inexpensive and versatile. They are not as messy as paints and thus are more easily controlled, particularly in classroom settings. Most importantly, young children love crayons and have a great deal of fun using them. With such an amazing combination of qualities, it's no wonder that crayons are one of the most widely used art materials in preschools and elementary schools.

History of the Crayon

The concept of using a tool for coloring and drawing dates from prehistory. The primitive crayon may have been an object as simple as a charred bone or hardened piece of colored clay. The precursors of modern crayons originated in Europe in the 1700s. These early crayons were sticks made from a mixture of charcoal and oil. Later, powdered pigments replaced the charcoal, and wax was substituted for the oil to make the sticks sturdier and easier to handle. However, early crayons were expensive, came in limited colors, and were mainly used by professional artists.

Today, the world's largest manufacturer of crayons is Crayola LLC, formerly Binney & Smith, which makes Crayola® crayons. The company started in 1885 as a partnership between cousins Edwin Binney and C. Howard Smith. One of the company's early products included the iron oxide pigment used in the classic red barn paint seen throughout much of rural America.

In 1900, Binney & Smith purchased a mill in Easton, Pennsylvania, to produce pencils from the abundant supply of slate in the area. Through its pencil-making business, the company saw the demand for inexpensive, high-quality school products and soon introduced the first dustless school chalk to America's classrooms. Next, the company set its sights on another teacher demand—good, affordable crayons.

Teachers at the time complained that school crayons were terrible. Crayons imported from Europe were of better quality but too expensive for a school budget. At the time, Binney & Smith was selling industrial wax crayons for marking crates and barrels. The ingredients in these wax crayons were not suitable for young children, who might be tempted to taste or eat the crayons. The company chemists were confident that they could replace the dyes used in the company's industrial crayons with a variety of safe pigments.

However, actual production of brightly colored, nontoxic crayons turned out to be more difficult than anticipated. Technicians had to hand-mix small batches of the liquid crayons to precise specifications to ensure color uniformity and consistency, while keeping costs low. According to the current Crayola website, "Special training and a blend of strength and gentleness were required to pull the slim [crayon] cylinders from their molds. Labels were rolled on by hand, another time-consuming process." *(www.crayola.com/mediacenter/HistoryOfCrayons.doc)*

In 1903, the company was ready to market its new brand of crayons. The product's name, Crayola, was suggested by Binney's wife, Alice, who combined *craie* (the French word for chalk) with oleaginous (which means oily). A pack of eight Crayola crayons sold for five cents and included the colors red, orange, yellow, green, blue, violet, brown, and black.

Over the years, Binney & Smith expanded the range of colors available and perfected its production process, although the carefully guarded formula is the same as it was in 1903. Crayola crayons now come in 120 colors, and the company produces nearly three billion crayons each year. *(www.crayola.com/mediacenter/CrayolaTrivia.doc)*

It is estimated that the average child in the United States wears down 730 crayons by his or her 10th birthday. Children aged two to eight spend an average of 28 minutes each day coloring, so it's little wonder that a study at Yale University found that the smell of crayons is one of the top 20 most recognizable odors to American adults.

How Crayons Are Made

At Crayola, formerly Binney & Smith, the first step in making a modern crayon is the creation of pigments. This process is done at a color mill, where water and various ingredients are mixed in large wooden tanks. The tanks are made of wood because metal would interfere with the chemical reactions that produce the color. Each pigment is made in a separate tank. After mixing, the color solution passes through a filter press to squeeze out excess water, leaving a moist cake of pigment that is broken into chunks and put into a kiln to dry for three to four days. The dried pigment chunks are then sent to blending machines to create different color shades. Next, the blended colors are ground into fine powders, which are bagged, weighed, and sent to the crayon manufacturing plant.

At the manufacturing plant, liquid paraffin wax is stored at a temperature of 190°F (88°C) in 17,000-gallon storage tanks. Large pipes transport the liquid wax to mixing vats where a predetermined amount of powdered pigment is added. The colored wax is heated to 240°F (116°C) and poured onto a rotating molding table that contains thousands of small cylindrical crayon molds. Pipes inside the molding table circulate water that is between 40°F and 70°F (4°C and 21°C) to cool the hot wax. Cooling times vary from four to seven minutes, depending on the color of the crayon.

The hardened crayons are hydraulically ejected from the molds, and the mold operator empties the crayons onto a worktable for inspection. Chipped or broken crayons are returned to the mixing vat to be melted and remolded. The accepted crayons are then transported by conveyor to an automated labeling machine that wraps and glues on the labels. This process is much faster than the hand-labeling method used in the early and mid 1900s. (During the Depression, farm families often hand rolled the labels in winter to supplement their incomes.) After labeling, the crayons are fed into packing machines that collate the colors into different box assortments for retail stores.

Waxes

The key to the success of the modern crayon is that it is made from wax. Waxes are soft, malleable substances with low melting points, which make them easy to mold into a variety of shapes. Waxes also adhere to a wide variety of surfaces, a trait useful in crayons. Most children's crayons today are made from petroleum-based paraffin wax. However, Dixon-Ticonderoga markets a soybean-wax crayon, and pure beeswax crayons are also available from different companies.

Waxes are a type of lipid, so they are fat-like in their properties. (Chemically, many waxes are esters of long-chain alcohols and fatty acids). However, the various substances we call waxes do not form a chemically homogeneous group, so the term is somewhat imprecisely defined. Natural waxes are mixtures of esters and may also contain hydrocarbons (hydrogen- and carbon-containing compounds with the general formula C_nH_{2n+1}). Many synthetic waxes are based on polyethylene.

Properties of the materials that we commonly classify as waxes include:
- malleable (can be easily bent or shaped without breaking) at room temperature,
- melting point above 113°F (45°C),
- insoluble in water, and
- hydrophobic (water repellent).

When people think of natural wax, they usually think of bees. The word wax is derived from the Old English *weax* for the honeycomb of a beehive. Bees produce wax to construct their honeycombs, which they use to raise their young and store their honey. Beeswax varies in color from nearly white to almost brown, depending on the types of flowers the bees visit. It has a relatively high melting point of 144°F–147°F (62°C–64°C).

Beeswax has been used and traded since ancient times and has been called mankind's first plastic. Its presence has been detected in the prehistoric paintings of the Lascaux cave in France. The Egyptians used beeswax in shipbuilding and mummy preservation. In classical times, nations paid tribute (a fee for protection) to the Roman Empire in beeswax. The Romans sent messages on hinged pairs of wooden writing tablets coated with beeswax. Pliny the Elder who lived from A.D. 23 to A.D. 79 mentions the use of white beeswax as a skin softener and an ingredient in broth to treat dysentery. In the Middle Ages, beeswax was considered valuable enough to be used as currency.

Today, beeswax is used to make candles and in cosmetics and pharmaceuticals. The *Waldorf Schools* incorporate beeswax as a key manipulative for young children to build coordination and fine muscular strength.

In addition to beeswax, other animal waxes include lanolin from the wool of sheep and spermaceti from the sperm whale. Lanolin is often used as a base for salves and ointments. Many waxes are also produced by plants. The most common vegetable waxes include bayberry wax from the bayberry plant and carnauba wax from the coating of Brazilian palm tree leaves. One of the most valuable of natural waxes, carnauba wax is used in car and floor polishes.

Paraffin wax was first isolated from crude oil in the 1850s. It is a mixture of saturated hydrocarbons with molecular formulas that range from $C_{18}H_{38}$ to $C_{32}H_{66}$. Paraffin wax is the main ingredient in household candles.

Many waxes today are synthetic. As supplies of certain natural waxes become depleted, research into new synthetic waxes has expanded over the last 50 years.

Because of their properties, waxes are useful in many manufactured products. Packaging is the most common use for wax, but other important markets include manufacturing of fire logs, tires, candles, construction materials, and cosmetics (including lipstick, mascara, and moisturizing creams). Wax is applied to corrugated cardboard and used in inks for computer printers. Wax is also used for covering cheese and for spraying fruits and vegetables on display in supermarkets. Wax is even added to the chocolate that we eat!

Household Products that Contain Wax

- wax paper
- paper cups
- furniture polish
- floor wax
- car wax
- candles
- dental floss
- shoe polish
- lip balm
- lipstick
- mascara
- body waxes
- hair wax
- food packaging
- candy corn
- jelly beans

References

American Chemical Society. *Chemistry in the National Science Education Standards: A Reader and Resource Manual for High School Teachers;* Washington, DC, 1997.

Ash, D.; Greene, C.; Austin, M. "Inquiry by Teachers," *Connect.* 2000, *13*(4), 12.

Barman, C.R. "Teaching Teachers: The Learning Cycle," *Science and Children.* 1989, *26*(7), 30–32.

Beisenherz, P.C. "Explore, Invent, and Apply," *Science and Children.* 1991, *28*(4), 30–32.

Bresnik, J. "Facilitating Inquiry," *Connect.* 2000, *13*(4), 6–8.

Chaille, C.; Britain, L. *The Young Child as Scientist: A Constructivist Approach to Early Childhood Science Education;* Allyn & Bacon: Boston, 2003.

Cheong, W. "The Power of Questioning," *Connect.* 2000, *13*(4), 9–10.

Connect: Inquiry Learning Issue. 1995, *8*(4), 1–20.

Connect: Inquiry Learning Issue. 2000, *13*(4), 1–26.

Crayola Website. About Crayola. Media Center. Crayola Trivia. www.crayola.com (accessed October 1, 2007).

Crayola Website. About Crayola. Media Center. History of Crayons. www.crayola.com (accessed October 1, 2007).

Cyberlipid Website. Waxes. www.cyberlipid.org (accessed October 3, 2007).

Dialogue on Early Childhood Science, Mathematics, and Technology Education; American Association for the Advancement of Science (AAAS) Project 2061: Washington, DC, 1999.

Eager to Learn: Educating Our Preschoolers; Bowman, B.T., Donovan, S.M., Burns, M.S., Eds.; National Academy Press: Washington, DC, 2001.

Edwards, C.; Gandini, L.; Forman, G. *The Hundred Languages of Children: The Reggio Emilia Approach to Early Childhood Education;* Ablex Publishing Corporation: Norwood, NJ, 1993.

Fat Chance—The Chemistry of Lipids. Sarquis, A.M., Ed.; Science in Our World Series Vol. 4; Terrific Science Press: Middletown, OH, 1999.

Gandini, L. "Fundamentals of the Reggio Emilia Approach to Early Childhood Education," *Young Children*. 1993, *49*(1), 4–8.

Gather.com Website. History of the Crayola Process. www.gather.com (accessed October 1, 2007).

Helm, J.; Beneke, S.; Steinheimer, K. *Windows on Learning: Documenting Young Children's Work;* Teachers College Press: New York, 1998.

The History Channel Website. History of Toy and Games. Crayons. www.history.com (accessed October 1, 2007).

Hoisington, C. "Using Photographs to Support Children's Science Inquiry," *Young Children*. 2002, *57*(5), 26–32.

Horn, G. *The Crayon;* Davis Publications: Worcester, MA, 1969.

HowStuffWorks Website. How Are Crayons and Markers Made? www.howstuffworks.com (accessed October 1, 2007).

Jones, J.; Courtney, R. "Documenting Early Science Learning," *Young Children*. 2002, *57*(5), 34–40.

Katz, L. "Impressions of Reggio Emilia Preschools," *Young Children*. 1990, *45*(6), 10–11.

Katz, L.G.; Chard, S.C. *The Contribution of Documentation to the Quality of Early Childhood Education.* ERIC/EECE Clearinghouse on Elementary and Early Childhood Education, 1996. www.ericdigests.org/1996-4/quality.htm (accessed January 24, 2008).

Kilmer, S.J.; Hofman, H. "Transforming Science Curriculum," *Reaching Potentials: Transforming Early Childhood Curriculum and Assessment,* Vol. 2; National Association for the Education of Young Children: Washington, DC, 1995: pp 43–63.

Lind, K. *Exploring Science in Early Childhood: A Developmental Approach;* Delmar Publishers: Albany, NY, 2000.

Lind, K. "Science in Early Childhood: Developing and Acquiring Fundamental Concepts and Skills." Dialogue on Early Childhood Science, Mathematics, and Technology Education. American Association for the Advancement of Science (AAAS), 1999.

Lowery, L. *The Biological Basis of Thinking and Learning;* Lawrence Hall of Science: Berkeley, CA, 1998.

Lowery, L. "How New Science Curriculums Reflect Brain Research," *Educational Leadership*. 1998, *56*(3), 26–30.

Lowery, L. *The Scientific Thinking Process;* Lawrence Hall of Science: Berkeley, CA, 1992.

Marek, E.A.; Cavallo, A.M.L. *The Learning Cycle: Elementary School Science and Beyond;* Heinemann: Portsmouth, NH, 1997.

Meisels, S.J., et al. *An Overview: The Work Sampling System;* Rebus Planning Associates: Ann Arbor, MI, 1994.

Moriarty, R. "Entries from a Staff Developer's Journal…Helping Teachers Develop as Facilitators of Three- to Five-Year-Olds' Science Inquiry," *Young Children.* 2002, *57*(5), 20–24.

National Association for the Education of Young Children (NAEYC). *Developmentally Appropriate Practice in Early Childhood Programs Serving Children from Birth through Age 8,* 1997. www.naeyc.org/about/positions/daptoc.asp (accessed January 31, 2008).

National Association for the Education of Young Children (NAEYC). *Guidelines for Appropriate Curriculum Content and Assessment in Programs Serving Children Ages 3 through 8.* Produced jointly with NAECS/SDE and NAEYC and adopted by both Associations in 1990. Published in *Young Children,* March 1991, pp 21–38 and in *Reaching Potentials: Appropriate Curriculum and Assessment for Young Children,* Volume 1, 1991, pp 9–27. *naecs.crc.uiuc.edu/position/currcont.html* (accessed January 30, 2008).

National Research Council. *National Science Education Standards: Observe, Interact, Change, Learn;* National Academy Press: Washington, DC, 1996.

Oz, C. *How Is a Crayon Made?;* Simon & Schuster: New York, 1988.

Reaching Potentials: Appropriate Curriculum and Assessment for Young Children, Vol. 1. Bredekamp, S., Rosegrant, T., Eds. Washington, DC: National Association for the Education of Young Children (NAEYC), 1992.

Reaching Potentials: Appropriate Curriculum and Assessment for Young Children, Vol. 2. Bredekamp, S., Rosegrant, T., Eds. Washington, DC: National Association for the Education of Young Children (NAEYC), 1995.

Selinger, B. *Chemistry in the Marketplace: A Consumer Guide,* 4th ed.; Harcourt Brace Jovanovich: San Diego, CA, 1989.

Snyder, I. *Wax to Crayons;* Children's Press: New York, 2003.

Villavicencio, J. "Inquiry in Kindergarten," *Connect.* 2000, *13*(4), 3–5.

Western Association for Art Conservation Website. WAAC Newsletter. Vol. 19, Number 3, Sept. 1997. Categories of Wax-Based Drawing Media. palimpsest.stanford.edu/waac (accessed October 1, 2007).